MAGIKCRAFT

ANCIENT WISDOM FOR THE MODERN PRACTITIONER

Lynn MagikCraft Swain

MAGIKCRAFT PUBLISHING LLC ✦ DURHAM, NC, USA

MagikCraft: Ancient Wisdom for the Modern Practitioner
© 2025 MagikCraft Publishing LLC

Creator, Author, Designer, and Editor: Lynn MagikCraft Swain
MagikCraft.com
Lynn@MagikCraft.com

Art Director, Editor, and Graphic Designer: Diana Robinson
dianawrobinson.com

Artist/Painter: C. Arianne Hemlein
@designsbyarianne

ISBN: 979-8-9994104-0-5

Published by MagikCraft Publishing LLC
1916 Perry Street
Durham, NC 27705 USA
MagikCraft.com, Lynn@MagikCraft.com

Welcome, Seeker of the Ancient Sacred Ways!

You now hold in your hands a grimoire, a companion, and a key to your Soul Goal: a living book of *Ancient Wisdom for the Modern Practitioner*. This work was born from countless hours of devotion — from the whispers of the ancestors and spirit guides, the fire of ritual, and the quiet moments of reflection where the veil between worlds grows thin.

It is not simply a book — it is a doorway and a portal into the mysteries of the goddesses, the guidance of the MagikCraft Oracle, runes, the wisdom of herbs, crystals, astrology, Sabbats, elements, lunar magic, and the eternal dance of moon and stars.

Within these pages you will discover spells, rituals, affirmations, and teachings designed to not only awaken your magic but also empower your spirit. You will walk beside Hekate, Morrigan, Cerridwen, Isis, Aphrodite, Lilith, Gaia, and beyond — each goddess revealing her gifts as you step into your own path of sovereignty.

Along the way, the chakras will guide you as inner gateways of energy and alignment; fairies will remind you of wonder, mischief, and elemental connection; and sigils will serve as symbols of intention etched into the fabric of reality. You will come to understand the soul mapping of both your literal and metaphorical journey, tracing the pathways of transformation that shape your becoming.

The cosmic blueprint of your own astrology will reveal itself as a celestial map, offering insight into destiny, rhythm, and divine timing. You will

learn to move with the rhythms of the cosmos, harness the alchemy of elements, align with your Soul Goal, and unapologetically embody your true power as both seeker and oracle.

This book is for practitioners, witches, wanderers, mystics, healers, and the curious soul who knows there is more to this world than what meets the eye. It is for you — here, now — ready to weave timeless traditions into modern practice and to stand in your power and claim the magic that has always been yours.

In opening this book, you are also walking with me in the Spiritus Mundi.

Your choice to hold this creation and welcome it into your sacred practice supports not only your transformation but mine as well. It is my honor to share this journey with you, and I offer you my deepest gratitude for allowing me to share my heart, my craft, and my vision through these pages.

May you find empowerment.
May you find healing.
May you find yourself.

This is your invitation to step fully into the circle of magic. The dragonfly hovers at the threshold, offering vision, transformation, and the reminder that belief itself is the spell.

Welcome, beloved seeker. The journey begins here for you to Stand in Your Power and Follow Your Soul Goal!

Lynn MagikCraft Swain

About the Author

Discover Your Soul Goal with Lynn MagikCraft Swain!

Lynn MagikCraft Swain is an internationally recognized psychic medium, author, intuitive coach, keynote speaker, and transformational teacher known for her powerful presence and life-changing guidance. Born in South Jersey, raised in England, and having lived across multiple East Coast states, Lynn brings a rich, worldly perspective to her sacred work.

A Duke University–certified life and career coach and Brian Weiss–trained past-life regression therapist, Lynn empowers individuals to navigate transitions, heal deeply, and align with their higher purpose. Her intuitive mastery is rooted in seven generations of mystic spiritual lineage and fused with decades of experience in corporate leadership and entrepreneurship.

Lynn's metaphysical shops have been honored with local "Best Of" awards every year from 2016 to 2025. Her work has been featured by major media outlets, including ABC and NBC, and she has received recognition from both Duke University and the University of North Carolina.

Whether guiding clients through a spiritual awakening, assisting in career shifts, facilitating past-life healing, or offering profound intuitive insight, Lynn is a trusted mentor devoted to helping others live their most authentic, empowered, and soul-aligned lives.

Gratitude

✦ *To the artist and painter* ✦

The visual essence of the MagikCraft Oracle deck was birthed through a sacred collaboration with artist **C. Arianne Hemlein**. Each painting was cocreated through intuitive dialogue and visionary exchange, blending my channeled descriptions, metaphysical symbolism, and personal family photos to ground the artwork in both lineage and lore. Working together over five years, Arianne skillfully transformed these visions into luminous, layered compositions that radiate emotion and magic. As an intuitive artist, she brought texture, depth, and divine resonance to every brushstroke. Our collaboration was an act of creative devotion, where art became portal and story became spell. *@designsbyarianne*

✦ *To the art director, editor, and graphic designer* ✦

Heartfelt gratitude to **Diana Robinson**, editor and graphic designer, with whom I have had the joy of working since February 2025. What a ride it has been — from early mornings to late nights and all the magic in between. Diana's creative devotion carried this project through countless transformations, from the first concepts to the final layouts. With unwavering patience, precision, and vision, she brought form to the formless and polished each page until it gleamed.

Diana, your hours of tireless creation — pouring your artistry into every detail from the cover to the spine and all in between — speak not only to your extraordinary expertise but to the ancient creative current flowing through your soul. You infused *Ancient Wisdom for the Modern Practitioner* with a living energy, shaping each page until it radiated with beauty and balance.

Your presence behind the scenes was both grounding and inspiring. This book carries your signature in every subtle border, every polished word space, and every shimmering alignment. I am beyond grateful for your patience, your brilliance, and the way you breathed life into these pages with creative energy that is nothing short of magical. Diana, thank you for walking this path with me, for holding the vision steady through every turn, and for illuminating the way with your gifted light. *dianawrobinson.com*

✦ To Megan and Erin Fasold, architects of this manifestation ✦

Through your company Elevate Me Consulting (*ElevateMeConsulting.com*), you did far more than support this project; you elevated and built the final business aspect of it beside me. With a shared vision and sacred determination, you poured passion and precision into every layer — from deep research into best practices and spiritual product trends, to crafting marketing models, contracts, pricing tiers, and launch readiness. Your fingerprints are etched into the soul of this creation. With every contract reviewed, workflow mapped, and spell whispered, you were there.

Your recognition that I needed to shift energy to complete this project, along with your invitation to the beach house at Emerald Isle, N.C., in March 2025, gave me space to pivot to the next steps. It was the last flame to ignite the final chapter of this five-year journey, the spark that breathed momentum and completion into this longtime vision. Through late nights, early mornings, and coffee-fueled brainstorms along with a few shots of Jack Daniels and unwavering devotion, you became visionaries, healers, and builders in one.

You are the business architects of this manifestation, and I am immeasurably grateful. You didn't just help launch a product, you helped call my dream and vision into being, like conjurers of destiny who summoned magic into form. You masterfully organized our Kickstarter strategy, meticulously managing timelines, logistics, deliverables, and backend systems all while holding the heartbeat with the newly created websites of *LynnMagikCraft.com*, *MagikCraft.com*, and *70Magic.com* steady and strong. You created order from chaos and cleared a path for my dream to manifest.

Megan Fasold, eighth-generation healer and my extraordinary daughter, you are the embodiment of the Solitary Practitioner card. Rooted in ancient knowledge, guided by intuitive brilliance, and ignited by radiant creativity, you illuminated every facet of this work. You led the complete redesign of my websites, infusing them with clarity, purpose, and soul. From technical mastery to energetic alignment, your ability to synthesize vision into form carried this project with grace, wisdom, and fire.

Erin Fasold, my brilliant daughter-in-law, your grounding presence and luminous business acumen transformed inspiration into elegant execution. You masterfully orchestrated complex moving parts and anchored the Kickstarter project in sacred structure and organization. You weaved the unseen threads, timelines, and numerous systems and legal layers of trademarks and copyrights, and with each wave of laughter we weaved threads of joy that strengthened our bond and amplified our blessings.

The Faces of the MagikCraft Oracle

✦ To each of you whose essence graces these cards ✦

Your presence is more than image. It is energy, lineage, and living archetype. You are not simply captured in art; you are woven into the spell — immortalized in a sacred language of light, shadow, and transformation. Your willingness to be seen, to embody both the mystical and the mundane, the goddess and the guide, breathed life into this oracle. You lent your eyes, strength, softness, truth, and authentic self, and in doing so you helped birth a magical portal through which others may heal, awaken, and remember. This deck could not exist without your courage, your soul's beauty, and your sacred yes. Thank you for standing as living mirrors of myth, memory, and magic.

Inner Child (#4), Bella Lynn Winston, *my beautiful great-granddaughter, 10th-generation practitioner, and pure magic in motion:* Your laughter sparkles with the wisdom of many soul lives. Your kindness, intelligence, and knowledge of magic light the path of all who know you. Bella, you awaken the inner child. You are stardust wrapped in love.

Ancestors man (#6), William "Billy" Bierbrunner Jr., *my brother and 7th-generation practitioner:* We have walked through fire and wonder, shadow and light, never letting go, bound by blood, love, and the ancient magic that sings in our veins. You are both my living kin and my ancestral bond, carrying the wisdom of those who came before us and reflecting it back to me with fierce loyalty and unshakable love.

Ancestors baby (#6), Robert James "Bobby" Thomas, *my brave great-grandson and 10th-generation practitioner:* You make me laugh from the soul and greet the world with a brave and curious heart. A true lover of nature, from frogs and insects to snakes and birds, you see the sacred in all creatures. You are a wild and wondrous joy to experience. I'm forever grateful for the magic you bring to my life.

The Journey (#7), Brayden Paul "Bray" Moran, *my first and only grandson and 9th-generation psychic, an intuitive soul with gifts as abundant as they are empowering:* May you boldly map your soul's journey toward a life full of purpose, love, and laughter, guided by your shining, intuitive, trustworthy frequency of light. From your athletic strength to your creative spark and quiet intelligence, you are one of the most powerful and gentle souls I have ever been honored and blessed to know. May you eternally sprinkle your magic.

The Bard (#8), Thomas William "Tom" Swain Jr., *my husband the storyteller, singer, artist, and philosopher of holistic medicine:* Songs flow from your cells and your soul. You awaken holistic wisdom through weaving a network of knowledge that awakens, soothes, and teaches. A lover of the natural world, golf, and other sports, you find peace and inspiration in open landscapes, sharing ancient knowledge with sacred intention and enthusiasm.

Solitary Practitioner (#9) Megan Lynn "Meg" Fasold, *my only birthed daughter of blood lineage and an 8th-generation practitioner and healer:* A beacon of autonomy, sacred rite, intelligence, and wild wisdom, you walk your path unapologetically with fierce authenticity, healing others while honoring the deep soul-knowing passed through your old-soul spirit. I am immeasurably proud of the woman you are and in awe of your strength, timeless wisdom, and radiant, positive energy. You are a spell spun in human form. You now carry the eternal torch, lit by lineage, burning with your own sacred fire. A force of nature, born of legacy, forged by choice, you are not only my daughter but also a living altar of our bloodline and a magical unique spell cast into the world.

Pandora's Box (#11), Nova Lynn Schuppan-Trout, *my granddaughter/daughter born through from my soul and 9th-generation practitioner:* A force of transformation, you carry the wild spark of rebellion and the sacred fire of truth. Serving in the Navy with honor to your country and family, you embody strength in motion, balancing service with soul, grit with grace. You are the one I can count on to intuitively create the altar and light the candle for me without my knowing. I am endlessly amazed by the vibrant, electric joy you bring into every space, a living reminder that power can laugh, dance, and dare all at once.

Goddess Cerridwen (#14), Doreen Ann Newsome, *my mom, truly the enchantress:* Your psychic abilities were breathtaking, from vivid dreams to clear-eyed mediumship. You walked between worlds with quiet command. I watched you heal with your hands. You held secrets that the veils and time couldn't hide and spoke to the ghosts that stood before you as clearly as any living soul. You would always say, "Goodbye and God bless," with a proclamation that left the room still. May your soul rest in peace. I forgive, though I do not forget.

Goddess Morrigan (#15) Annie Hunter Church, *my nanny (grandmother):* In silence you could hold a room — your deep, dark brown eyes staring into souls with a knowing that arrived before your voice ever did. With your worn poker deck, you read the future through cartomancy, offering truths wrapped in European superstitions, yet undeniably real. You would pause, sigh, and mutter, "Ehhh, yaa bugs," with that exasperated expression I came to cherish, just before revealing a hard truth or sharp insight. You were my heroine as a child — shrouded in mystery, rooted in power, and unforgettable in spirit.

Goddess Lilith (#16) Kimberly Ann "Kim" D'Agostino, *my youngest sister:* Our bond is non-negotiable. You are the freedom seeker and the wild heart who runs with horses, communes with birds, and curls up with cats like old friends. A brilliant psychic and gifted fashionista with a designer flair that is indisputable, you are a radiant testament to your sovereign, intuitive power. Magic pulses through every spell you speak and every glance you give — a living lineage of mysticism.

Goddess Isis (#17) Nahal Kaivan de Lalondriz, *doctor, witch and healer:* You are the one who knows me better than anyone on this planet — my soul's soft landing. Your beauty radiates, your intelligence sharpens every space, and your sensual, spirited energy leaves a trail of magic wherever you go. More than a friend, you are my sister witch, my spiritual daughter, my chosen kin across lifetimes, and knowing you is one of my greatest joys. I knew you were important to me the moment I met you buying your witchy supplies at MagikCraft.

Goddess Gaia (#19), Shelley Lynn Thomas (Schuppan-Trout), *my granddaughter/daughter:* Etched into the stars and sealed by soul, you entered my life as a surprise at just 17 days old. Your ancient soul spoke to mine within seconds, a silent recognition that echoed through lifetimes. You are the embodiment of Gaia: mother of four, teacher of many, inspiration wrapped in nature's grace. With your feet always bare upon the earth, you are magic made manifest, a living spell of presence. Your being hums with a quiet medicine, vibrating healing into the world simply by existing. I am endlessly proud of the woman you are.

The Sigil (#36), Justin Scott Turner, *trusted mentee, employee, spiritual son, and fellow practitioner:* Our journey began when you were a teenager. Over the years you have forged yourself into a true magus — one of will, precision, and poetic power. This sigil you created is more than ink or symbol; it is a key of intention, a seal of knowing that your hands and intentional gift you created for me. It breathes your spirit and awakens the blessing. It is a vessel of power and devotion that now lives within the MagikCraft Oracle. Thank you!

William "Bill" Bierbrunner Sr., *my dad:* Born and raised on the shores of South Jersey, you carry the grit of the coastline and the calm wisdom of the tides. From serving in the Air Force to a life of hard work and exploration, you have lived with purpose and heart. Your love of nature, land, and history flows through me. Your honest words, rock-solid values, and willpower to never give up has helped shape who I am. You taught me there are no strangers on the road — only friends waiting to be met. In your 90th year, your strength humbles me. You are a portal woven from threads of timeless magic, and I am honored to be your daughter.

This dragonfly symbol is not merely a logo.
It is the living sigil of the sacred threshold.

With wings of light, the dragonfly hovers at the
veil—where shadow meets radiance
and illusion gives way to sight.

The eye above its center sees
through realms, dimensions,
and lifetimes.

This is the portal of the dragonfly—the
passageway into truth, transformation, and
timeless magic.

When you gaze upon this glyph, you are
being summoned

not to believe, but to *remember*;
not to follow, but to *awaken*.

Enter. Initiate. Emerge.

You are the key and the threshold.
Cross over, and reclaim your wings.

The Cards

How to Use the MagikCraft Oracle................................4

1. Believe................................8

2. Psychic Medium................................14

3. Chakra Alignment................................20

4. Inner Child................................26

5. The Elements................................32

6. Ancestors................................38

7. The Journey................................44

8. The Bard................................50

9. Solitary Practitioner................................56

10. Runes................................62

11. Pandora's Box................................68

12. Spiritus Mundi................................74

13. Goddess Hekate................................80

14. Goddess Cerridwen................................86

15. Goddess Morrigan................................92

16. Goddess Lilith................................98

17. Goddess Isis................................104

18. Goddess Aphrodite................................110

19. Goddess Gaia..116

20. Moon Phases...122

21. Cosmic Blueprint..128

22. Aries: The Ram...134

23. Taurus: The Bull...140

24. Gemini: The Twins......................................146

25. Cancer: The Crab..152

26. Leo: The Lion...158

27. Virgo: The Virgin..164

28. Libra: The Cauldrons...................................170

29. Scorpio: The Scorpion.................................176

30. Sagittarius: The Centaur............................182

31. Capricorn: The Sea Goat.............................188

32. Aquarius: The Water Carrier.......................194

33. Pisces: The Fish...200

34. Celtic Wheel of Life....................................206

35. The Dragonfly..212

36. The Sigil...218

How to Use the MagikCraft Oracle

Your MagikCraft Oracle is a sacred tool of reflection, vision, and intention. Each card is a portal, and each spread is a conversation with the unseen. The following are three core practices to begin your journey or deepen your existing ritual.

Dragonfly Seven-Card Spread

This in-depth spread is designed for deeper insight, energetic mapping, and intuitive alignment. It reflects your spiritual ecosystem and the many facets of a soul question.

Card Positions:

1. Essence — Your current energetic state
2. Challenge — What is testing or blocking your flow
3. Support — Resources, allies, or inner strengths
4. Desire — The heart of your longing or intention
5. Action — What to do, shift, or choose next
6. Lesson — What your soul should be integrating
7. Outcome — The potential result or energetic result

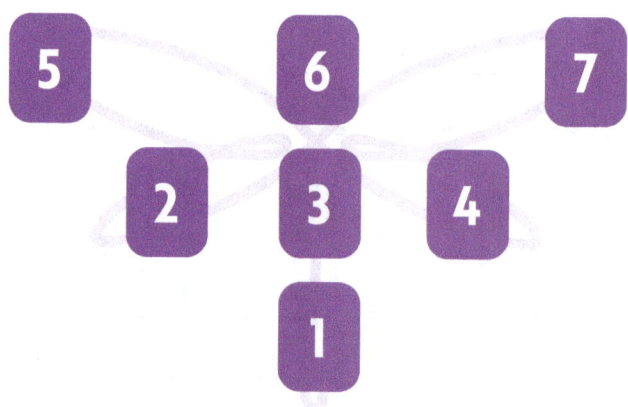

The MagikCraft Oracle's Dragonfly Seven-Card Spread awakens awareness and ignites transformation, guiding you to soar into your next chapter of life.

The Daily MagikCraft Oracle One-Card Meditation

This is a simple and powerful way to connect with your inner knowing and the energy of the moment. Use as a daily ritual, during a moment of indecision or energetic overwhelm, or to support a journaling, meditation, or intention-setting practice.

How to Use:

· Take a quiet, deep breath, thinking positive in and negative out as you center yourself.

· Ask a question such as, What do I need to know right now?

· Shuffle the deck, and pull one card.

· Reflect on the card's message, colors, symbols, and guidebook meaning. Allow your intuition to speak first.

The MagikCraft Oracle Three-Card Spread

This spread reveals the story you are currently living through. It reflects your recent path, your current energy, and the doorway opening ahead.

Card Positions:

1. Past — The lesson, pattern, or energy you are moving away from

2. Present — Where you are now and what is being revealed

3. Portal — What is being offered, invited, or becoming

Enhancements:

· Place a crystal or herb bundle beside the cards.

· Light a candle or candles to focus your attention.

· Write a reflection based on the card's energy.

The Veil Walker Spiral

This spread is designed to guide the seeker through a spiral of awareness, unveiling what lies beneath, within, and ahead. It honors the cyclical, spiral nature of magic, transformation, and soul remembrance. It is ideal for moon phases, seasonal turning points, or shadow journeys.

Lay the seven cards in a spiral formation, beginning in the center and curving outward clockwise.

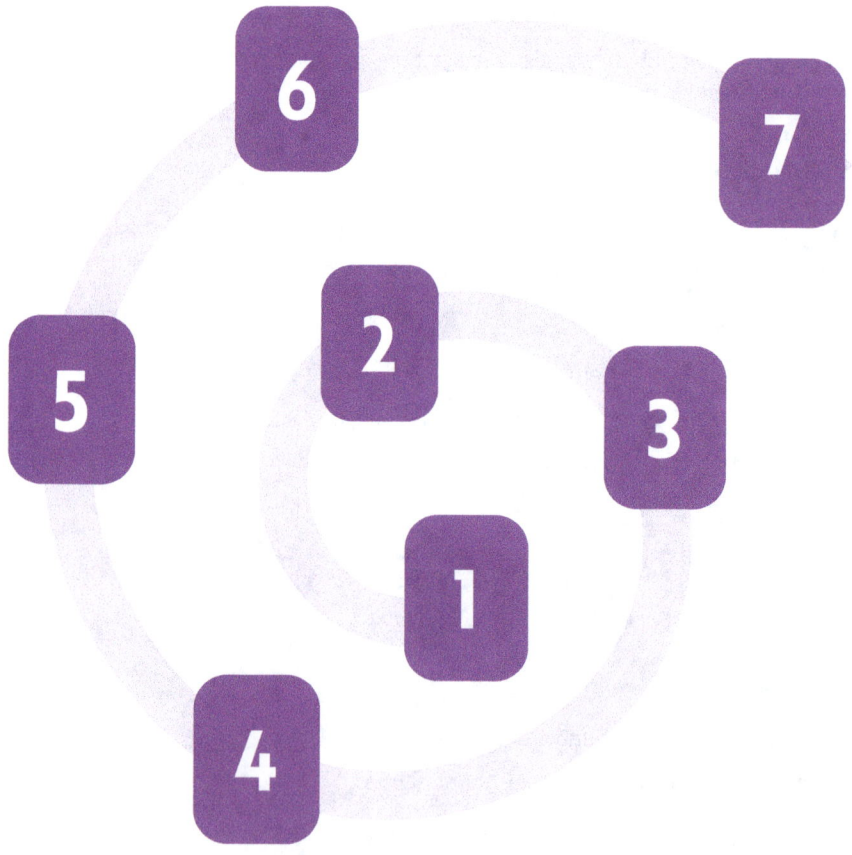

Card 1: The Center Flame
Position Meaning: Your inner light at this moment
Purpose: Anchors the spread; reveals your core energy or truth being activated
Destined Path: Use cards rich in *Essence, Invocation,* or *Soul Goal.*

Card 2: The Rooted Veil
Position Meaning: What you are not seeing clearly
Purpose: Reveals illusions, hidden fears, or distorted beliefs; the veil that is ready to be lifted
Destined Path: Cards with *Shadow* or *Subconscious* themes work well here.

Card 3: The Liminal Call
Position Meaning: The spirit, dream, or unseen force that is speaking to you now
Purpose: Channels insight from your higher self, guides, ancestors, or dreamworld
Destined Path: Look to cards with *Oracle, Symbolism,* or dreamlike imagery.

Card 4: The Threshold Key
Position Meaning: What must be surrendered or unlocked
Purpose: The doorway to your next becoming; requires release, risk, or ritual
Magik Thread: This is powerful for cards with *Transformation, Alchemical Spell,* or *Sacred Disruption.*

Card 5: The Spiral Rising
Position Meaning: Your sacred strength rising
Purpose: The gift, lesson, or medicine spiraling upward from within you now
Destined Path: Draw on cards with *Empowerment, Crystals,* or *Invoked Power.*

Card 6: The Path of Embodiment
Position Meaning: How to walk your magic in the world
Purpose: Offers a spell, action, or way of being to ground your soul path in reality
Destined Path: Ideal for *Ritual, Earth,* or *Mystic Frequency* entries

Card 7: The Outer Ring (Vision Unfolding)
Position Meaning: What lies on the horizon if you step through the spiral
Purpose: Shows the energy of integration, outcome, or destiny available as you complete the spiral
Destined Path: Choose cards with *Prophecy, Soul Flight, Oracle,* or cyclical themes.

Essence:

Magical Energies
Invocation
Stand in Your Power
Follow Your Soul Goal

Dragonfly Echo

I stand at the threshold of the unseen, grounded in trust and lit by the fire of belief. I honor my intuition as sacred truth and my dreams as divine guidance. I invoke my power with knowing, not fear. Even in uncertainty, I choose to remember who I am, even if to others it is unseen. My belief is the spell that opens the way.

I. Believe

Energetic Invitation: Step into the threshold — the liminal space between what is and what could be. You may not see the outcome, and that is where the magic lives. This moment asks you to trust in the unseen, to listen to the quiet knowing in your bones, and to honor the visions your heart sees before the world does.

You are invited to believe in the magic that already surrounds you — in the multiverse unfolding through signs, symbols, and synchronicities. Belief is not passive. It is a sacred act of power that calls energy into form. When you trust, you align with unseen allies and open portals of possibility.

Use your tools: Hold your crystals to anchor intention. Light your candles to call in clarity. Lay your cards to reveal the whispers of Spirit. Open your sacred books to awaken memory. These are not props; they are conduits of connection — keys that unlock your inner temple and attune you to divine rhythm. Your intuition is real. Your dreams are transmissions. Your rituals are bridges between dimensions.

This card invites you to remember that you are both seeker and source, spell and spark. Your dreams are not random. Your intuition is not a mistake. These are transmissions from your higher self. Speak your truth. Light your own path.

Belief is the spell that begins it all. Believe in the multiverse. Believe in the mystery. Believe in yourself. Stand in your power, and trust your Soul Goal. Your magic is real.

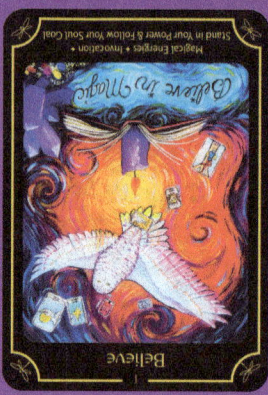

Shadow Path

When the Believe card appears in reverse, it arrives not as punishment but as a sacred pause, a soul echo, or a mirror. Doubt is not the enemy of belief — it is the invitation to go deeper. This moment is asking you to sit with your uncertainty, to let it reveal where your soul goal has been clouded by fear or fatigue.

You are not behind. You are not broken. You are in a spiritual recalibration. Even luminous spirits lose sight of their flame. This card reminds you to come back to your magical energies, to tend your altar — internal or external — and to reconnect with what you once knew to be true. Forgetting is part of the remembering. Let this be a return to trust of yourself and the magic that is available to all who seek it!

Symbolic Vision: A white owl soars across a swirling, multidimensional sky with her wings outstretched on winds of Spirit, gliding between the veils of the seen and unseen. She is the silent sentinel, a sacred messenger who carries the memory of ancient wisdom and the echo of magic that never left this world. Her golden eyes gleam like portals, reflecting truths long buried yet still alive within the soul.

Around her, tarot cards dance through the air like whispers from the cosmos, each one a sacred invitation to trust your intuition and step fully into your mystical knowing. Below, a flickering flame rises atop an ancient, open book. This is no ordinary text — it is a soul codex, a living manuscript glowing with divine light. Its pages are written not in ink, but in experience, devotion, and cosmic memory. Each word is a spell, and each paragraph a prayer.

This book is your sacred scripture — your story unfolding in real time, alive with the magic of your becoming. It does not preach rules; it remembers the truth. It teaches that belief is not passive — it is the force that activates the unseen. When you believe, the words glow brighter. The book breathes.

To the side, a crystalline temple rises from the earth — spires of amethyst, quartz, and moonstone are arranged in sacred geometry. These are not decorations; they are consciousness carved in mineral form. They hum with purpose, amplifying your energy, clarifying your intentions, and reflecting your soul goal back to you with radiant precision. These crystals are guardians of vibration — alive, awake, and aligned with the frequencies of healing, clarity, and remembrance. In their presence you do not ask for proof — you feel the resonance of truth. This vision is not fantasy; it is a mirror.

The owl is your intuition. The book is your sacred memory. The flame is your focused light. The crystals are your clarity and intention. The tarot cards are your dialogue with the divine. Everything here whispers the same message: It is in the hush of dawn, in the breath between thoughts, and in the spark that rises when you trust without evidence.

Magic is not something you must create — it is something you allow. It is the ancient energy flowing through trees, books, rivers, stones, and breath. It is the rhythm of your heart when you speak your truth. It is the presence that surrounds you when you remember who you are. To believe in magic is to awaken to the truth that you are not separate from the divine — you are the divine, dreaming yourself awake.

You are the owl, the scribe, the flame, the crystal. The spell is already cast. Believe in magic. It is real. It is here. It is alive. It is you!

Sacred Reflection

What am I being asked to trust, even without it being seen today? Belief is the spell that precedes evidence. This question calls you to surrender to the unseen, honoring that intuition often knows before the world reflects it.

Ritual

Awakening the Magic Within and Around You

Supplies

- A crystal that calls to you (such as amethyst for intuition, rose quartz for heart wisdom, or obsidian for protection)
- A magical or spiritual book that shaped you or one you want to explore
- A candle (white, gold, or purple for truth, vision, and divine light
- An image, feather, or token representing the owl or your chosen animal spirit guide

Step 1: Set Your Intention.

Gather your ritual elements, and intentionally place them before you. As you arrange them, whisper, *"I invite sacred allies to walk with me. This space is blessed. This moment is mine. I believe."*

Step 2: Call Upon the Spirit Guide.

Close your eyes, and breathe deeply. Visualize the white owl — silent, wise, and luminous — gliding into your space. Or imagine the animal spirit that resonates with your soul. Whisper or speak, *"Sacred guide of feather, fur, or flame, show me the magic within my name. Reveal what is hidden. Anchor what is true. Awaken the wisdom that lives in all I do."* Feel the presence of your guide settle near you, like a witness and as allies to your becoming and believing.

Step 3: Ignite the Flame of Knowing.

Light your candle slowly and with intention. As the flame flickers to life, say, *"This flame is the light of my remembering, transmitting and receiving. May it ignite my inner magic and illuminate the path I am ready to walk."* Let the glow wash over you. Imagine it lighting up every forgotten corner of your inner temple.

Step 4: Activate the Crystal.

Hold your chosen crystal in both hands. Close your eyes, and let your breath sync with its energy. Feel its vibration. Ask it to amplify your belief and awaken the sleeping gifts within you. Whisper, *"I charge this crystal with truth and trust. Anchor my knowing. Expand my sight."* Place it beside your candle to absorb the flame's energy.

Step 5: Open the Magical Book.

Take your book — whether one well-loved or a book you are learning from and resonate with — and hold it to your heart. Say, *"This book holds keys to realms within and beyond. Let its words unlock wisdom I already hold and wisdom that I may not know."* Open the book to a random page. Let the first sentence or paragraph you see be your sacred message. Speak it aloud, and then reflect: Why this message? What stirred within you?

Step 6: Declare the Spell of Belief.

Place your arms in the air fully stretched upward and outward and speak this declaration or create your own: *"I believe in the magic that lives in my bones and in the unseen threads I follow home. I believe in spirits, signs, sigils, and soul. I believe in myself. I am whole."* Visualize this belief rippling outward into your field, summoning synchronicity, clarity, and alignment.

Step 7: Offer Gratitude, and Close the Circle.

Thank your animal guide, your book, your crystal, and your candle. Bow to yourself in reverence. Gently extinguish the flame and say, *"The ritual is complete, but the magic lives on — within me, around me, always."* Hold the crystal or the book close one last time. Let this be your anchor when doubt arises. You have touched the threshold and returned with power.

Essence
Sacred Power
Divine Transmission
Oracle
Transcendent Wisdom
Seer

Dragonfly Echo

I am a sacred channel of transcendent wisdom, guided by Spirit and rooted in truth. I trust the unseen, for it speaks through me from beyond the sacred veil. I walk the sacred path with wisdom, trust, and authenticity and with my third eye open.

2. Psychic Medium

Energetic Invitation: This card calls you to remember who you are: a vessel of knowing, a translator of the invisible, a sacred bridge between realms. Your intuition is not a whisper of doubt — it is a voice of truth echoing through time. The Psychic Medium card arrives when your intuitive gifts are stirring, reawakening, or seeking deeper integration. You are being invited to embody your role as a sacred channel — a mystic who delivers messages from Spirit to the seen world. You are not merely receiving visions. You are the transmitter of visions.

You carry transcendent wisdom, guided by Spirit and rooted in truth. The energy that flows through you is not random — it is divine transmission. When you feel tingles, sense presence, or hear the whisper, trust the voice, symbols, signs, and sensations that arrive. They are sacred messages carried across the veil. You are an oracle, an instrument of sacred power, born to translate the unseen and walk between worlds. This gift lives in your bones and breath, waiting for your presence and permission to flow.

You walk the sacred path with wisdom, trust, and authenticity and with your third eye open. The unseen speaks through you, and your ability to hear it is an ancient remembering. Spirit guides move beside you, working in harmony with your inner knowing. Through your devotion to truth and willingness to listen, you become a living bridge — a sacred channel of messages not yours to hold, but to deliver. Now is the time to reclaim your role, trust your knowing, and embody the deep remembering of who you truly are.

Psychic Medium
2

Sacred Power • Divine Transmission • Oracle
Transcendent Wisdom • Seer

Shadow Path

When reversed, this card may indicate hesitation, fear, or disconnection from your intuitive power. Perhaps you have doubted your role as a messenger. Perhaps you have softened your truth to stay safe or have dismissed sacred signs as coincidence.

This card reminds you that you are not making it up — you are remembering. You were never meant to fit in; you were meant to see beyond.

Reconnection begins with breath. Inhale trust. Exhale fear. Place your hands over your heart and third eye. Feel yourself return.

Let your path be devotional, not performative. Let your gift be honored, not hidden.

Symbolic Vision: Beneath a swirling twilight sky, a blonde-haired woman sits beneath the stars at a weathered table, cloaked in purple and wrapped in presence. She is not alone, though she sits in stillness. The air hums. The unseen gathers.

Cards are fanned within the crone's palm — each one a portal; each one a whisper. Beside her a sigil-inscribed candle flickers, its flame dancing like a beacon of intention. A luminous crystal ball glows from within, refracting the mysteries of realms beyond.

At the base of an ancient, spiraling spirit tree, mushrooms rise like small altars — symbols of ancient and ancestral wisdom, underworld knowing, and earthborn magic. A raven watches from above, nestled in the tree's limbs — a timeless messenger between worlds.

A sleek black cat sits at the medium's feet with its eyes wide with silent vigilance, acting as both companion and guardian. Overhead, the crescent moon glows with ethereal radiance, casting light on the glimmering stars — waypoints across the spirit sky.

This is no ordinary scene. This is a sacred rite, an act of divine transmission, and a communion across the veils. The medium does not guess; she receives. She does not seek control; she opens to the current. Through breath, vibration, presence, and deep listening, she becomes the conduit.

You are the seer. You are the oracle. You are the one who walks with spirits and energies from other dimensions and speaks their perceived truths. You listen not with ears, but with your soul. You see not with eyes, but with your inner knowing. You speak not just in words, but also in vibration and energy. You are the sacred channel. You are not simply reading signs — you are the sign. The veil parts in your presence.

When you step into this role, you do so with reverence, humility, and sacred power. You do not command the spirits; you commune. You are the living altar of divine wisdom, a mystic torchbearer, and a vessel of transcendent guidance. This card reminds you that being a psychic medium is not a performance — it is a responsibility. You are the bridge between worlds, the voice through which Spirit speaks, the hand that holds the message, and the heart that anchors light in the shadows. You are the veil-lifter.

You are the oracle, the one the ancestors whisper through. Now it is your time to receive all dimensional communications for transmission to yourself and others for whom the messages are issued. Everyone is a psychic medium. The gift lives within your bones, your breath, and your soul memory. The channel is already there — it only asks to be opened. The signs are waiting. The messages are nearby. It is time to listen. It is time to receive!

Sacred Reflection

How do my guides, ancestors, or unseen allies make themselves known to me? Reflect on signs, synchronicities, dreams, symbols, or sensations. Notice patterns. Do specific beings, feelings, or messages return? How do they speak through the veil?

Ritual

Oracle of the Veil: Opening the Psychic Channel

Supplies

- Space cleansers (sage, palo santo, or lavender)
- A candle (indigo, violet, or white)
- A crystal (amethyst, labradorite, moonstone, smoky quartz, amazonite, selenite, or clear quartz)
- A sigil of psychic activation

Step 1: Create the Sacred Circle.

Begin by cleansing your space with smoke and calling in the four directions. Cast a physical or energetic circle. Place your MagikCraft Oracle deck, a candle, and a sigil of psychic activation on your altar. Set your intention by saying, *"I open this space to divine presence, sacred power, and transcendent wisdom."*

Step 2: Anchor the Seer Within.

Sit comfortably, and close your eyes. Place the crystal over your third eye or in your left hand. Breathe deeply. As you exhale, whisper, *"I am the seer. I am the oracle. I open to receive divine transmission."* Feel yourself merging with your inner mystic. Visualize violet light spiraling from above, bathing you in cosmic intelligence and activating your intuitive senses.

Step 3: Light the Flame of Transmission.

Light your candle while gazing into the flame with soft focus. Say aloud, *"By this flame, I awaken the spark of divine sight. By this light, I open to sacred communication. May this candle carry my request to the realms beyond."* Imagine the flame becoming a beacon, illuminating the channel between dimensions.

Step 4: Activate the Sigil Gateway.

Place your hand over your drawn or printed sigil. Breathe life into it by saying, *"I empower this symbol as a gate of divine reception. Let it open the flow of transcendent wisdom and truth."* See the sigil glowing and pulsing. This is your psychic key.

Step 5: Draw from the MagikCraft Oracle.

Hold your deck to your heart. Ask a question or simply open to what Spirit most wants to convey. Shuffle slowly, and then draw one to three cards. Lay them before the candle. Gaze at the imagery, and speak aloud anything you receive — images, words, sensations, or ancestral whispers. Trust the knowing that rises. You are not imagining — you are remembering.

Step 6: Channel and Write.

Take your journal and begin to write what you receive. Let the voice flow through you with messages for yourself or for others. This is your divine transmission, spoken through your hands. This step anchors the spiritual into the physical, turning light into language. Include your interpretation of the oracle cards and any symbols, insights, or intuitive phrases you hear or feel.

Step 7: Seal the Wisdom, and Give Thanks.

To close, hold the crystal in both hands and say, *"I honor the spirits, guides, and energies who walked with me. I seal this sacred power within my soul and carry it with reverence. I am the oracle. I am the seer. I am the vessel of transcendent wisdom."* Blow out the candle, touch your forehead, heart, and the earth. Gently fold the veil. The messages will remain.

Optional additions:
· Use a sound bowl or chime at the beginning and end of the ritual.
· Trace the spiral symbol in the air to amplify the channel.
· Repeat nightly for seven days under the moon to deepen your psychic attunement.

Essence
Spiritual
Soul
Energy Vortex
Coherence
Resonance
Frequency

Dragonfly Echo

My energy flows freely.
I am aligned in body, mind,
and spirit. Self-alchemy
guides my transformation.
I am in balance with the
flow of universal energy.
Each chakra is open and
receiving divine love. I am
a radiant pillar of light.

3. Chakra Alignment

Energetic Invitation: This card arrives as a radiant affirmation: You are a living temple of light, and your energy centers are awakening in harmony with your highest path. Your chakras — spinning wheels of intelligence and illumination — carry the wisdom of your physical, emotional, and spiritual essence across lifetimes. With each breath you attune more deeply to your energetic rhythms, flowing like sacred rivers of light through the temple of your body.

Each chakra speaks with its own voice, guiding you toward clarity, vitality, creativity, and embodiment. Alignment is not perfection — it is presence. It is the quiet knowing that your energy system is alive, intelligent, and in motion. Like the phases of the moon or the tides of the sea, you are always shifting toward your next becoming. This card marks a sacred activation — a portal of recalibration where your inner compass tunes to truth.

You are invited now to explore your balance of self, recognizing where energy is overactive, undernourished, or harmonized. Chakra work is not a fix — it is a celebration. Each center is a sacred instrument in your divine symphony. Feel your roots deepen, your heart expand, and your voice open. This is the song of your wholeness.

Your soul goal is not to ascend beyond the body, but to fully embody your essence. Spiritual energy is not separate from physical form — it pulses through you, awakening the remembrance of your multidimensional nature. Trust your body. Trust your energy. You are luminous. You are whole.

Chakra Alignment

Shadow Path

When reversed, Chakra Alignment may indicate a disconnection from your body, emotions, or spiritual center. You may feel scattered, numb, depleted, or overwhelmed. Perhaps your energetic rhythms are disrupted — rushing when rest is needed or stagnating when movement calls. A lack of spiritual energy may feel like burnout or cynicism.

You may be ignoring your soul goal or chasing external achievement instead of turning inward. Balance of self can slip when one chakra dominates, such as overthinking without feeling. Activation becomes agitation rather than illumination when we bypass presence.

This is not judgment; it's a reminder to return to yourself. You are not broken. You are evolving. Breathe in light. Exhale what no longer serves.

Symbolic Vision: A silhouette meditates in lotus pose, grounded in spiraling water, rooted by vibrant lotus petals, and crowned by divine light.

Behind the still form, a tree of life stretches upward, its branches swirling like sacred currents in the wind of the cosmos. The air shimmers with the presence of unseen forces, as if stars are whispering their memory into matter. Time itself feels suspended.

At its zenith hovers a dragonfly, delicate yet potent — a symbol of transformation and the guardian of energetic balance. Its wings flicker with ancestral knowing, hovering between dimensions.

Each curve of light, each petal of the lotus, and each ripple of water speaks of movement and sacred intention. You are not simply sitting within alignment;

you are the alignment. You are a temple of light — a symphony of subtle frequencies. You are the spiral of soul and matter dancing in harmony.

Your body hums with spiritual energy, vibrating through seven sacred spheres. When the chakras align, the energetic body becomes a radiant field of coherence. This balance of self refines your frequency, tuning your soul goal to divine pitch. You become both the seeker and the silence, the current and the calm. You are the resonance between body and cosmos.

From the root, the pulse begins — deep, red, and anchoring. It speaks of belonging and grounding in the earth. Here, your sense of safety is activated, and your energetic rhythms find their first beat.

The sacral flows orange with sensuality, creativity, and emotional waters. It is the seat of feeling, intimate connection, and inspired motion. This is where your desires swirl with passion and become sacred art.

At the solar plexus, golden light radiates from your center. Confidence and power rise here — the fire of will igniting action. Empowerment pulses in your belly like the sun at high noon, awakening your soul goal in the world.

The heart, in vibrant green, blossoms open. Compassion breathes here — love that is both inward and expansive. Your essence softens and stretches to meet the world in kindness. This is the portal of presence.

Blue light shimmers at the throat, where truth becomes word and vibration. Your voice becomes a spell of liberation, and the energetic rhythm of honest expression pulses through every sound.

At the third eye, indigo insight unfolds. Vision opens like a petal blooming at dusk. Here, clarity is activated — not just of sight, but also of knowing.

Above all, the crown radiates violet light — a beacon of spiritual connection. Divine wisdom pours in like starlight. You remember you are the temple. You are the light.

Sacred Reflection

Which chakra feels most open today, and which feels blocked or needing care? Notice this in your emotions, body, or choices. How might balance feel? What color, sound, movement, or affirmation could help realign and support this energy center?

Ritual

Chakra Activation

To awaken, align, and harmonize the seven sacred energy centers through embodied ritual and intention, this ritual invokes your inner rainbow, activating the flow of divine energy through your being.

Supplies

- *Seven candles, crystals, or objects in chakra colors (red, orange, yellow, green, blue, indigo, violet/white)*
- *A reflective crystal, such as clear quartz, labradorite, or selenite*
- *A journal and pen*
- *Optional: tuning fork, singing bowl, chakra music, or essential oils*

Step 1: Root Chakra – I Am Grounded.

Represents safety, stability, primal trust, connection to Earth, and the physical body
Place your hands over the base of your spine. Visualize deep red light glowing and spinning. Say, *"I am grounded. I am supported by Earth and ancestors. My foundation is strong and sacred."* Breathe into the soles of your feet. Feel yourself anchored in the now.

Step 2: Sacral Chakra – I Am Creative.

Represents emotions, sensuality, pleasure, fluidity, and creative expression
Place your hands just below your navel. Envision a glowing orange current, warm and flowing. Say, *"I feel deeply. I embrace sacred pleasure. I flow with the waters of life."* Sway gently, allowing your body to move like water.

Step 3: Solar Plexus Chakra – I Am Empowered.

Represents willpower, confidence, personal truth, action, and transformation
Place your hands on your stomach. Visualize bright yellow light radiating like the sun. Say, *"I am strong. I take inspired action. I burn away all doubt in the fire of my power."* Feel your core ignite with courage and purpose.

Step 4: Heart Chakra – I Am Love.

Represents unconditional love, compassion, forgiveness, and divine connection
Place your hands over your heart center. Visualize lush green or soft pink light expanding outward. Say, *"I love and am loved. My heart is open and whole. I radiate grace."* Let a breath of gratitude rise and fall with your heartbeat.

Step 5: Throat Chakra – I Am Truth.

Represents authenticity, communication, expression, sound, and vibration
Gently touch your throat. Envision a clear blue light swirling at your neck. Say, *"I express myself freely. My voice is sacred. I speak spells of truth and clarity."* Let a sound rise from within — a hum, chant, or name.

Step 6: Third Eye Chakra – I Am Vision.

Represents intuition, insight, perception beyond the veil, and spiritual awareness
Rest your fingers on your brow between your eyes. Visualize deep indigo light pulsing with quiet knowing. Say, *"I see the unseen. I trust my inner vision. My intuition is my guide."* Hold your reflective crystal to your third eye, and gaze inward.

Step 7: Crown Chakra – I Am Divine.

Represents unity, consciousness, enlightenment, connection to Source
Lift your hands slightly above your head or place them gently on your crown. Envision violet or white light flowing like starlight. Say, *"I am open to divine light. I receive wisdom from the cosmos. I am one with all that is."* Feel yourself as a channel between heaven and Earth.

Closing Words

Bring your awareness to the full column of light within you. Imagine all seven centers humming in harmony. Say, *"I am the living current. My chakras are aligned, my path is clear, and my spirit is radiant. So it is above as below."* Hold your reflective crystal close. Seal your energy field. Journal any insights, sensations, or symbolic visions.

Essence

Whimsical

Enchanted Wonder

Alchemy of Joy

Soul Remembrance

Dragonfly Echo

I embrace the wonder, the wounds, and the wisdom of my inner child. I choose to live with open-hearted joy. I am healing generational patterns by loving the young self I once was. I rekindle spiritual play and explore magic with a youthful heart. I spin barefoot on the Earth and sit upon the water to reflect.

4. Inner Child

Energetic Invitation: This card is a sacred summons to remember who you were before the world told you who to be. When the Inner Child appears, it calls you back to your original rhythm, where laughter echoed in every corner and joy was your native tongue. It is a mirror reflecting your soul remembrance, reminding you that your essence has never been lost; it is only tucked away beneath layers of time and expectation.

You are invited to reconnect with the wild, unfiltered magic of your youth — to awaken the spark of enchanted wonder and dance again with the curiosity that once shaped your world. Let go of perfection. Return to the messy beauty of imagination. Reclaim your right to sing to the moon, bask in the sun, skip barefoot through dew-soaked fields, and color outside every line.

This card may arrive during a time of emotional healing. Wounds from early life — moments when you were still learning what it meant to be safe, seen, and loved — are rising to be acknowledged, cuddled, soothed, and gently reparented. In this sacred pause, your alchemy of joy becomes medicine. Laughter is your potion. Play is your ritual. Creative freedom is your balm.

You do not need to become someone new. You are being called to remember who you truly are. That whimsical, radiant soul still lives inside you, with arms outstretched and heart wide open.

Let your magic come home. Let your smile return like sunrise. Let your inner child lead you forward.

Whimsical • Enchanted Wonder •
Alchemy of Joy • Soul Remembrance

Inner Child

4

Shadow Path

When reversed, this card may
reflect disconnection from joy
or suppression of old pain. You
might be denying your softness or
shielding your heart out of fear or
pressure to perform.

Has your Inner Child been silenced
for the sake of responsibility or
perfection? You may need to grieve
what you did not receive or give
yourself now what was once denied.

You are still allowed to believe in
joy. Your inner child is not a ghost
but rather your guide.

This reversal is a call for radical
compassion: You are worthy
of delight. You are worthy of
remembering.

Symbolic Vision: A golden-haired
child fairy kneels in soft grass
beneath a twilight sky, where magic is
not simply remembered   —
it is lived. Her
iridescent wings
unfurl behind
her like petals of
starlight, echoing
the innocence,
radiance,
and divine soul
remembrance of her being.

She wears a flowing white dress,
handwoven from organic hemp
— a sacred fiber connecting her
to Earth's purity and
elemental wisdom.
Embroidered
over her heart is
the triple moon
symbol, a lunar
glyph holding
the essence of
maiden, mother, and
crone. It speaks to the eternal cycle
of becoming and reminds you that
even in the tender heart of the child
lies the wisdom of lifetimes.

A crown of fresh daisies rests upon
her golden head — symbols of joy
and innocence and a portal to the
fae realms. Around her, glowing orbs
spiral skyward — tiny starlit beings
and etheric guides. They represent
spirit fairies, multidimensional
magic, and the unbroken thread

between your highest self and child self. These orbs are not simply light — they are enchanted wonder, the alchemy of joy, and whisperings of healing across time. They shimmer like constellations reborn, reminding you that you have always been held, even in your most fragile moments.

Before her lies a quiet, mirror-like pond. It reflects not only her image but also an ancestral memory — a deeper soul frequency rising through shimmering water. As you gaze into its depths, you are invited to retrieve sacred glimpses of joy and moments of wonder, laughter, and awe that once lived in your bones — the first time you chased butterflies, sang in the rain, or believed in something unseen. These memories are not lost; they are crystalline fragments waiting to be retrieved. The pond becomes a portal of remembrance, activating truths stored in your cellular memory. Through it, you glimpse the child you were before the world told you who to be as well as the soul you are becoming.

This child fairy is not merely a dream — she is a beacon of divine memory. Her essence stirs the light within that knows how to sparkle without apology. She reminds you that your laughter is sacred, your joy is medicinal, and your innocence is not a weakness — it is a superpower. She is the untamed muse of your original magic, the one who turned shadows into lanterns and wounds into wisdom.

You are invited to reclaim your playfulness, to color outside the lines, skip down moonlit paths, and sing to the wind. For when you choose play, you choose healing. When you remember your inner child, you rewrite your story.

Sacred Reflection

When was the last time I let myself catch fireflies, blow bubbles, or laugh from my belly without apology or judgment? What kind of freedom or magic lives in that moment, and how can you bring more of it into your days?

Ritual

Inner Child Wonder and Play

Supplies

- A daisy crown or flower garland
- Bubbles or a bubble wand
- A bowl of water or a childlike mirror
- Sidewalk chalk, crayons, or paints
- A sweet treat (such as honey, berries, or organic candy)
- Firefly-safe space or candlelight to represent them
- Bare feet, open sky, and a playful heart

Step 1: Circle of Wonder

Choose a grassy patch, garden, or meadow, if possible. Using chalk, stones, petals, or wildflowers, draw a spiral or circle on the earth. This is your sacred play space — your portal to wonder. Step inside barefoot and whisper, *"I enter the sanctuary of my inner child. I welcome home joy, light, and magic."* Let the breeze kiss your cheeks and the earth root your feet. Feel safe. Feel seen.

Step 2: Crown and Spin of Remembrance

Place your daisy crown or flower garland on your head. If outside, skip joyfully to gather blossoms, and then spin in loose, wobbly circles with arms out and heart open. Let your hair fly. Laugh from your belly and say, *"I honor the child who danced in me before the world grew loud. I return to lightness."* Remember that spinning, skipping, and silliness are sacred movements.

Step 3: Bubbles of Blessing

Blow bubbles into the open air. With each breath, release joy into the world. Imagine each bubble as a sparkling spell carrying wishes, laughter, and magic. Say, *"Each bubble is a joy spell. Each breath is a laugh reborn."* Chase them. Pop them. Be enchanted by their dance.

Step 4: Firefly Glow and Reflection

or by candlelight, imagine fireflies glowing around you. Gaze into your bowl of water or mirror and whisper, *"Little lights of wonder, return to me."* Ask softly, *"Dear inner child, what joy have we forgotten?"* Allow a memory, image, or emotion to surface. Let it be gentle. Let it be true.

Step 5: Art of the Heart

Grab paints, chalk, or crayons. Scribble, smear, or swirl color onto paper, the sidewalk, or your skin. There are no rules, just fun. Say, *"This is the magic language of my inner child. I create without judgment."* Laugh if you spill. Smile if it gets messy. Be wild in your expression.

Step 6: Song and Sweetness

Sing anything you love — a childhood lullaby, a made-up tune, or your favorite pop song. Let your voice be joyful, silly, off-key, or bold. Then slowly savor your honey, berries, or chosen sweet. Say, *"My voice is the lullaby of return. This joy is mine."* Taste the sweetness, and let it stir wonder awake within you.

Step 7: Declaration and Release

Stand tall in your circle and say, *"I am magical, wild, and free. I am the guardian of joy."* Blow out your candle, wave goodbye to the fireflies, and step barefoot out of the circle — renewed, delighted, and deeply connected to your inner light.

5. The Elements

Essence

Roots of Earth
Breath of Air
Flow of Water
Flame of Fire
Spirit Compass

Dragonfly Echo

I honor the elements within and around me. I am in balance with Mother Nature's forces and walk in sacred rhythm with earth, air, fire, water, and spirit. Rooted like quartz in the north, I rise with the breath of the east, ignite in the fire of the south, and flow through the waters of the west. Anchored, inspired, transformed, and whole — I am nature's magic embodied.

Energetic Invitation: This card calls you back into harmony with the primal forces of creation: earth, air, water, fire, and spirit — the five elemental powers forming the architecture of the physical and energetic world. Each reflects a unique part of your being. When balanced, they empower your body, heart, voice, intuition, and vitality. When misaligned, you may feel confused, flooded, disconnected, overworked, or stuck. Earth grounds, water flows with emotion and intuition, fire ignites courage and transformation, air inspires thought and voice, and spirit weaves them into a compass of soul.

Honor the elements of Mother Earth as both sacred forces and wise teachers. Earth teaches you to root, build, and trust your foundations. Air reminds you to breathe, speak, think clearly, and shift perspectives. Fire fuels passion, energy, and the courage to rise and transform. Water asks you to feel deeply to release and surrender to the flow of emotion. Spirit reminds you that you are never separate — you are the living thread that connects all things.

Embracing the elements is a path to integration. Walk outside barefoot. Light a candle with intention. Breathe with awareness. Cry when the tide calls. Meditate with crystals. Dance in the rain. These acts awaken elemental harmony in your soul-body. You are not just in nature — you are nature.

This card invites realignment. Ask yourself, *"Where am I rooted? Where am I drifting? What needs cleansing? What wants to burn bright? What wisdom is the wind whispering?"* This is a sacred pivot — a call to ritual, nature, and embodiment.

Shadow Path

When The Elements card appears reversed, you may feel directionless, energetically scattered, or overwhelmed. One or more elemental energies may be dominating or neglected: Overwork or burnout may signal too much fire. Emotional overwhelm may reflect an excess of water. Mental noise or overthinking may indicate too much air. Stagnation or heaviness may mean too much earth.

This card asks you to pause and listen to what each element needs to say. Step outside. Breathe. Touch the soil. Light a candle. Let water soothe. Let air clear. Invite Spirit to help you recenter.

You are not lost. You are remembering how to listen.

Symbolic Vision: A bold black-and-white compass rose spins at the heart of the card, rooted in sacred geometry and nature's direction. It is surrounded by radiant quadrants of elemental color and force.

North (green, earth) is crowned with quartz crystals and the glyphs of Taurus, Virgo, and Capricorn. Anchoring, stabilizing, and nourishing, the roots of earth remind you to ground your purpose and stand steady in your truth.

East (yellow, air) is illuminated by wind and white sage smoke, flowing with the symbols of Gemini, Libra, and Aquarius. This is the breath of air, bringing mental clarity, inspiration, and the sacred exchange of ideas and truth.

South (red, fire) is ignited with flame and candlelight and infused with Aries, Leo, and Sagittarius.

This quadrant burns with the flame of fire — desire, courage, willpower, and divine transformation.

West (blue, water) is awash in moonlight and the gentle curve of waves. At its center rests a chalice, glowing with emotion, intuition, and the sacred feminine. This is the flow of water, where feeling, memory, and psychic depth move through you like tides of truth.

In magical tradition, each direction represents not only a physical orientation but also a spiritual gateway — a frequency, current, or magical intelligence that responds when honored. When you cast a circle, call the quarters, or create an altar, you are inviting the powers of earth, air, fire, and water to hold sacred space, protect your intention, and amplify your spellwork. The elements help align your inner reality with universal law. They are not static. They are dynamic forces of creation and transformation.

North is often evoked for grounding, protection, stability, and manifestation spells. It governs physical resources, ancestry, and the bones of the earth.

East brings new beginnings, clarity, divination, communication, and the winds of change. It rules the mind, language, and inspiration.

South ignites passion, ambition, purification, and energetic power. It is the spark that fuels courage, banishes fear, and energizes will.

West is the realm of healing, dreamwork, shadow integration, and the mysteries of intuition. It supports rituals of release, emotional flow, and psychic awakening.

Together, these forces form a living elemental compass for the soul. This wheel does not just turn with the seasons — it turns within you. When you align with the elements and their sacred directions, you become the spell, the staff, and the star. You are the spirit compass, and every choice you make becomes a ritual in motion.

You are not separate from these forces — you are these forces. You are the altar. You are the ritual. You are the compass, turning ever inward to find your direction. Let earth steady you. Let water flow through you. Let fire fuel your courage. Let air lift your voice. Let spirit guide it all home.

Sacred Reflection

Which element do I feel most connected to in this moment, and how does it live through my body, emotions, or intuition? Let that element speak through sensation, memory, or imagery. What is it teaching you right now?

Ritual
Elemental Embodiment

Supplies
· Access to an outdoor area
· A feather or incense
· A candle
· Bowl of water or a nearby body of water

Step 1: Earth — Grounding the Body

Stand or sit barefoot on the ground. Close your eyes, and breathe deeply. Place your hands on your belly or hips. Affirm, *"I root into the wisdom of the Earth. I am safe, supported, and stable."* Feel the solidity beneath you. Imagine roots extending from your feet deep into the soil. Earth teaches presence, patience, nourishment, and the power of standing firm. Feel the pulse of nature below, steady and ancient.

Step 2: Air — Awakening the Mind

Wave a feather, light incense, or feel the breeze against your face. Take three conscious breaths, inviting clarity and expansion. Affirm, *"I breathe with awareness. I release the mental clutter and welcome insight."* Air carries ideas, truth, and the freedom to shift perspective. Let it clear the mind and inspire expression. Let it sing through you like wind through trees.

Step 3: Fire — Igniting the Heart

Light a candle, and gaze into its flame. Place your hand over your heart and feel its warmth and rhythm. Affirm, *"I honor the flame within. My passion and power rise with purpose."* Fire fuels transformation, courage, desire, and creative life force. Embrace its spark to awaken your will and inner radiance. Let its light illuminate your next becoming.

Step 4: Water — Softening the Soul

Sit near water, hold a bowl, or imagine waves flowing around you. Anoint your heart and third eye with water. Affirm, *"I trust my emotions. I surrender to the flow of my sacred waters."* Water invites feeling, dreaming, releasing, and intuitive knowing. It soothes, cleanses, and opens the heart. Let it carry away what no longer serves.

Step 5: Spirit — Weaving the Whole

Stand with arms open wide or palms upward. Feel the space around you and the invisible threads connecting all things. Affirm, *"I am the breath between the elements. Spirit moves through me in every moment."* Spirit is the center, the ether, the unseen force of life and soul essence that binds everything in harmony. In silence, feel the sacred rhythm of oneness.

Step 6: Embodied Element Walk

Go outside, and spend time with each element. Touch the earth. Breathe deeply in the open air. Feel the warmth of sunlight or a flame. Listen to or touch flowing water. Pause in stillness to sense Spirit's presence. Affirm, *"I meet the elements as kin, embracing their wisdom through my body and senses."* Let nature become your temple, teacher, and mirror.

Step 7: Closing Blessing

Hold a stone, feather, flame, drop of water, or any natural token. Place it on your altar or heart. Whisper, *"Blessed be the elements within me. I walk in balance, reverence, and wonder."*

Essence
Spirit Guides
Soul Imprint
Ancient
Bloodline
Rooted Wisdom

Dragonfly Echo

The strength that runs through my bones is ancient. The courage I need is already in my blood. I honor those who came before me. I walk with their wisdom, strength, and blessings. When I direct my mind's eye, they gather nearby. I walk with the strength of my ancestors. I am their living spell. I create a new lineage. Together, we co-create.

6. Ancestors

Energetic Invitation: You are being called into sacred remembrance — a deep reconnection with the energies that formed you long before this moment in time. This card is an energetic threshold that beckons you to listen with your whole being, to awaken your cellular memory, and root into the wisdom of your lineage.

Your bloodline holds more than genes — it carries ceremony, sorrow, resilience, and sacred gifts. You are the echo of those who endured, the breath of those who loved, and the dream of those who walked before you. Their messages speak not in language, but in rhythm — through synchronicities, sensations, and symbols that stir something deep within.

In honoring this rooted wisdom, you become the living altar — an embodiment of ancestral memory through which energy flows forward. You are not disconnected; you are the continuation.

Your soul imprint is unique, etched across lifetimes and vibrating with the essence of who you have always been. This signature frequency is shaped by experience yet remains undiminished. When you slow down, its song stirs within your heart, calling you gently back to your truth.

Your spirit guides walk with you now as guardians of your unfolding path. They do not shout. They whisper. Their language is intuition, and their presence is the steady pulse of love guiding you home.

You are the convergence of the ancient and the eternal, the seen and unseen, a vessel of divine memory shaped by time and carried by light. Trust what moves through you. It is remembered and sacred.

Shadow Path

When the Ancestors card appears reversed, it may indicate a disconnection from your roots or resistance to inherited patterns. Perhaps you feel burdened by ancestral trauma or distant from family ties. You may also be neglecting the spiritual allies who wish to support you.

This card asks, What wounds am I healing for my lineage? What wisdom am I meant to reclaim?

Even if you never met them, your ancestors know you. You are their prayer answered. Call to them. Offer your presence. Be the cycle breaker, the story bearer, and the sacred bridge.

Symbolic Vision: This image is a sacred tapestry rich with spiritual symbolism and layered meaning. At its heart stands a magnificent willow tree, its verdant tendrils cascading like curtains of memory. The willow is a universal symbol of intuition, healing, remembrance, and the sacred art of bending without breaking. It is the tree of the shamanic ancestors, mystics and healers.

The willow is not merely a backdrop — it is the axis mundi, the sacred tree of life, through which timelines spiral and souls return. Its roots drink deep from ancestral memory, while its branches brush against unseen realms. It shelters what is ancient and what is yet to be, holding both wisdom and wonder beneath its limbs. Its curved trunk speaks of strength shaped by surrender — a living gateway between dimensions.

To the side of the tree sits the elder ancestor. Cloaked in earth tones, he watches in stillness with a soft twinkle in his eyes. He is memory embodied — the quiet guardian of story, spirit, and time. He does not speak aloud, but he radiates presence. He is the timeless one who waits, who knows, and who holds the threshold for those who dare to remember.

Opposite him, a child plays barefoot in the deep meadow grass. His tiny feet press into the living earth, unfiltered by shoes or worry, responding instinctively to the rhythm below. He does not seek magic — he is magic. His laughter stirs the veil. His innocence opens the field.

Around him, dragonflies swirl in luminous spirals, acting as spirit messengers.

The dragonfly is a symbol of transformation and the crossing of dimensions. It weaves between seen and unseen, carrying prayers from earth to ether. Its iridescent wings shimmer with truth: Nothing dies; everything shifts. Where the dragonfly appears, soul evolution is near.

The orbs that float through this card are memory seeds — ancestral echoes responding to the joy of the child and the gaze of the elder. Together, they activate a sacred circuit: past, present, and potential, held in one illuminated moment.

The soul is eternal. It moves through seven dimensions of soul life, each a realm of remembrance, healing, and expansion. Ancestors reside within these planes as protectors and teachers. Whether through the stories of their physical lives or their unseen guidance, they shape your path with signs, dreams, and presence.

This card is not just a moment in a meadow. It is a living portal. The child awakens the field, the elder keeps the gate, and the willow holds them both.

Sacred Reflection

Whose ancestral strength do I carry in my bones, even if I have never known their name? Reflect on the unseen threads of courage and wisdom that may live within you from your ancestral line.

Ritual

Ancestral Visualization

Supplies
- A willow branch, leaf, or image to represent the portal and tree of life
- Dragonfly imagery or token to call in transformation and spirit messengers
- An ancestor photo or item to place nearby in reverence if you wish to call forth a known family presence
- A candle

Step 1: Create the Grove

Find a quiet space. Place a small bowl of water near your feet, and light a candle nearby to honor spirit. Close your eyes, and envision a great willow tree before you, with its tendrils swaying like curtains of time. This is your portal. Stand or sit beneath it in your mind's eye.

Step 2: Root Into the Earth

Place your bare feet flat on the ground. Breathe deeply. Imagine roots unfurling from your feet, burrowing into the rich soil. Feel your body become still and steady. Say aloud, *"I open myself to remembrance. I root into the sacred ground of all who walked before me."*

Step 3: Call Forth the Elder

Visualize the elder ancestor arriving at the base of the willow, cloaked in quiet wisdom. Greet him with reverence. Ask inwardly, *"What memory do I carry that was once yours?"* Be open to images, emotions, or silence. Trust what comes.

Step 4: Invite the Inner Child

Now see the child entering the grove, playful and barefoot, laughing among orbs of light. Allow your own inner child to join. Let them touch the tree, run in the meadow, or sit with the elder. This sacred reunion begins to awaken the ancestral seeds buried in your being. It soothes, cleanses, and opens the heart. Let it carry away what no longer serves.

Step 5: Receive the Dragonfly

Visualize dragonflies swirling around you in luminous spirals. These winged messengers fly between worlds. Ask one to land in your palm. Whisper a prayer or question into its wings, and then release it skyward, knowing your message is carried beyond the veil.

Step 6: Plant the Seed

Take a small object — such as a stone, crystal, or written intention — and place it at your feet or on an altar. Whisper, *"I plant this seed in honor of the souls in the dimensions. I remember. I receive. I rise."*

Step 7: Return with the Light

When ready, open your eyes. Journal what you felt, saw, or remembered. The ritual is complete, but the connection remains. Your ancestors now walk more closely with you. The willow still stands within, and the dragonfly still carries your spirit between the worlds.

Essence

Wanderlust

Spiritual Motion

Expansion

Sacred Passage

Odyssey

Dragonfly Echo

I place my soul in motion.
Guided by wanderlust,
wonder, and spirit-led
compass, I trust the path
unfolding. Each step is a
spell; each mile is a quest.
I cross thresholds with
courage and release what
no longer serves my soul.
My journey is sacred across
lands or within spirit.
I welcome expansion,
surrender to change, and
follow intuition home.

7. The Journey

Energetic Invitation: You are invited to put your soul in motion. The Journey card arrives when your inner or outer world is shifting — when wanderlust becomes more than a desire. It stirs as a sacred hunger to move beyond the known. Whether you are preparing for a trip, sensing an internal shift, or facing a life change, you are being summoned into sacred movement. This is a moment of spiritual motion, where every step forward becomes part of your unfolding path.

Travel, whether physical or mystical, reshapes you. It stretches perception, opens the heart, and dissolves resistance. If you have felt stagnant, restless, or unsure, know that expansion is already underway. Something within you is reaching for new terrain — new choices, new truths, or new freedom.

You are crossing a threshold and stepping into a sacred passage that will transform your direction and deepen your awareness. Let go of the need to control the route. The road ahead is being revealed moment by moment through the art of soul mapping — navigating by dreams, signs, and intuitive trust.

Let curiosity lead you. Let wonder guide your feet. Wanderlust is the spark that ignites the flame of transformation. Every mile walked and every change embraced becomes a sacred imprint on the evolving map of your spirit.

You are not lost. You are arriving — again and again — into the becoming of your true self.

Every breath and every mile becomes a mantra of transformation. Let intuition be your compass, and let wonder be your guide.

Wanderlust • Spiritual Motion • Expansion •
Sacred Passage • Odyssey

The Journey

7

Shadow Path

The shadow side of the Journey reveals resistance to movement, fear of change, and the illusion of safety in stagnation. You may cling to what is familiar, even when it no longer nourishes your spirit. The call to explore might trigger anxiety, avoidance, or overwhelm — rooted in past disappointments or fear of losing control. Unhealed trauma, ancestral beliefs, or rigid routines may hold you back from embracing the unknown. Wanderlust may turn into escapism, or spiritual motion may feel directionless without grounding.

This card invites you to open your imagination and dream beyond the edges of your current reality. Where have you limited yourself?

To heal, begin mapping your soul's desires. Listen deeply, trust expansion, and allow growth, even when the direction isn't fully known.

Symbolic Vision: A barefooted teenager stands at the edge of the world, where land yields to sea and sky opens wide in breathless invitation. Before him stretches the great ocean, not just of water, but also of possibility. This is no ordinary moment. It is the soul's turning point, a sacred pause before transformation — a breath caught between the self that has been and the one still becoming.

His body is a compass, with one arm reaching toward the shimmering horizon, the other hand gripping a black wrought iron railing. This railing is not a barrier but an anchor — solid, weathered, and ornate. It is a symbol of grounding, strength, and the beautiful tension between surrender and support. In spiritual tradition, wrought iron is said to repel negativity and maintain energetic boundaries. Here, it serves as a stabilizer between the known and the unknown. Even in sacred risk, we may reach for something true.

He is not lost; he is aligned — not waiting, but listening. The word across his chest reads Ascension —

not a destination, but a devotion. It's a vow to rise and meet life as both student and steward of the path. The ocean before him becomes a mirror of the soul — vast, ancient, and alive with memory. It does not promise escape, but return to spirit, joy, and origin.

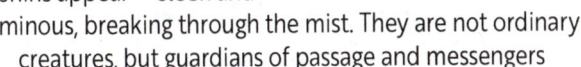

This is wanderlust in its truest form — the call to step into the odyssey of becoming. The horizon is not a limit, but a promise — a mapless invitation into spiritual motion, where movement becomes medicine.

From the depths, dolphins appear — sleek and luminous, breaking through the mist. They are not ordinary creatures, but guardians of passage and messengers of the in-between. Dolphins move between worlds. Their joy is sacred, and their presence is a song of thresholds. They teach us that healing can be graceful and laughter, divine.

The dolphin does not force; it flows. It does not analyze; it senses. Its essence is communion and clarity. To witness it is to remember: You are not here to be perfect. You are here to be present — to trust, to feel, to laugh, and to leap when the tide calls.

This is the essence of expansion — the sacred discomfort of growth. It is the shimmering edge of awakening, the breath before the leap. You are within a sacred passage, woven through the tides.

You are the compass. You are the tide. You are the rhythm between what was and what is rising.

Wherever you go, the soul of the ocean travels with you. The threshold is open. The dolphins carry your song.

Sacred Reflection

If I am the path, the compass, and the unfolding map, what chapter is being written right now? This is your soul speaking to itself. Let your pen become the channel. Name the energy, title the chapter, and describe the landscape of your becoming.

Ritual

Aligning the Inner and Outer Journey

Supplies

- A compass (real or symbolic)
- A map (travel map, hand-drawn journey path, or spiritual soul map)
- A white or gold candle
- A journal or sacred paper
- A stone or crystal (clear quartz, labradorite, or moss agate)
- A bowl of water (to represent emotional depth and flow)
- Optional: a token or charm that represents protection for travel

Step 1: Create the Sacred Circle.

Set your map before you, and place the compass at its center. Light your candle and say aloud, *"I open this circle as a vessel for movement, meaning, and magic. I call in guidance, clarity, and courage. May this map become a mirror. May this compass awaken what is true."* Take a few deep breaths. Allow your body to root and your heart to open.

Step 2: Activate the Compass Within.

Hold the compass in your hand. Turn slowly, aligning yourself with each of the four directions. Speak softly, *"North, show me my wisdom. South, reveal my fire. East, grant me new vision. West, carry my healing."* Now place your hand on your heart and whisper, *"And center, anchor me in trust."* Feel yourself aligning with both the magnetic and mystical pull of true direction.

Step 3: Trace the Journey on the Map.

Gaze at your map. This may be a literal location or a metaphorical one — drawn or imagined. Mark where you are now. Mark where you are going. Then draw or trace the path between them. Say aloud, *"Every step, seen or unseen, is part of my becoming. I bless this path with presence, devotion, and grace."* You may write words or symbols — such as courage, rest, transformation, and return — along the route.

Step 4: Write the Soul Itinerary.

In your journal, list three things you wish to take with you on this journey (for example, confidence, openness, and faith) and three things you choose to leave behind (such as fear, control, and doubt). Say, *"I release what weighs me down. I carry only what serves my soul."* Fold this list, and place it under your crystal or stone.

Step 5: Perform the Water Blessing of the Horizon.

Dip your fingers in the bowl of water, and anoint your third eye, heart, and soles of your feet. Say, *"As the dolphin swims between worlds, so shall I travel with fluid grace. Let me move through change as water moves through stone — cleansing, softening, and reshaping."* Gaze into the water, and see the horizon of your journey. Feel it beckoning you forward.

Step 6: Speak the Traveler's Vow.

Place your hands on the map and say, *"Wherever I go, I carry the sacred within me. I do not walk alone. My path is blessed. My compass is attuned to truth. My journey is a prayer in motion."*

Step 7: Close the Circle and Begin Again.

Gently blow out the candle and say, *"The threshold is open. The path is blessed. I begin again as both traveler and guide."* Carry the compass or map with you — or keep it on your altar — as a talisman of direction, intuition, and soul alignment.

Essence

Poet

Storyteller

Singer

Author

Musician

Artist

Nomad

Dragonfly Echo

I am a vessel of creativity and sacred expression. My voice is a spell, and my story a bridge between worlds. I carry the rhythm of the bard — the poet, the singer, the nomad, the artist. I do not wait for permission. I create. I remember. I rise. I am the magic.

8. The Bard

Energetic Invitation: The bard walks the path of the nomad, gathering tales from the wind, songs from the stars, and memories from the land. Every step is a stanza; every silence, a verse. This is a sacred call to live as both poet and pilgrim, letting your life become compass and canvas.

This card awakens your inner artist and storyteller — the one who weaves truth into form. The bard is not bound by medium. They are the musician who plays the unseen rhythm, the poet who conjures emotion into spell, and the keeper of both ancient and emerging lore.

You carry the books of knowledge written in your soul's ink, filled with stories only you can tell. Your journey, shaped by travel both worldly and spiritual, becomes a library of sacred memory.

Let your hands paint what your heart knows. Let Spirit sing through your voice. Your words are spells. Your stories are seeds. Your presence is a living poem.

The Bard card reminds you that your experiences are not random — they are verses of the sacred song you came to share. Speak them. Sing them. Write them. Dance them. Let the earth hear your music. Let the stars echo your truth.

You are not just inspired. You are the voice of inspiration itself. The pen is your wand, and the page, your altar.

You are the bard — the one who carries the song of the soul across time. You are the storyteller, the wanderer, the weaver., and the keeper of light hidden in language.

The Bard

Shadow Path

When the Bard arrives reversed, it whispers of silenced voices and dimmed colors. You may find yourself questioning the validity of your expression — feeling like a muted instrument in a world too loud or a sacred book left closed. Self-doubt might twist your artistry into shame or your nomadic spirit into perceived instability.

This shadow stems from a legacy of repression. Perhaps you were taught that art must be practical, that music must make sense, or that beauty must be justified. But these are not your truths. You are the author now, and the quill belongs to you. The reversal is a soft knock saying, *"Remember who you are. You were born to create. Your voice is the bridge, not the barrier."* Reclaim your rhythm, even if your voice trembles. It is sacred.

Symbolic Vision: A cloaked elder stands barefoot on a field of dewy grass beneath the soft veil of twilight. His presence hums with ancient rhythm, as if the land itself recognizes him.

In one hand he holds a crimson leather-bound book etched with the word *Bard*. It pulses with memory — its living pages echo the sacred tales of poets, singers, storytellers, and artists from every age and village. These are the visionaries and mystics who dared to channel the divine through creativity. Their words, songs, and dances became oral histories, spoken and sung from town to town and country to country, stitched into the songlines of collective memory.

In his other hand, the elder leans upon a wooden staff, worn smooth by many pilgrimages. At its crown rests an ancient amber crystal sphere, glowing like captured sunlight — radiant, warm, and alive. This sacred stone, a fossilized resin of trees long gone, is the bard's flame — the solar fire of inspiration and the crystallized essence of healing, ancestral wisdom, and life force. It lights the path for those brave enough to speak their truth, even when the world resists listening.

Above his head spins the triskelion, with its spiraled arms turning like a divine metronome. This sacred symbol marks the dance of body, mind, and spirit — the creative current through which the bard channels expression. The body acts and moves, the mind shapes vision into form, and the spirit breathes meaning into the work. Through this triad, the bard becomes a vessel of living myth.

Beyond the hilltops, verses lie waiting to be sung. Sacred stones hum with ancestral tones, vibrating with forgotten melodies. The bard's journey does not end here. He crosses the seas and walks the moors, meadows, villages, and towns — each step a prayer and each path a verse. From misty cliffs to sun-drenched fields, he carries the book of knowledge to all who will listen.

He travels across borders and through ages, his voice bringing teachings wrapped in song, poetry, and myth. At every village fire, coastal shrine, forest circle, and temple threshold, he shares stories that awaken memory and magic.

You are no longer the observer. The elder smiles — not with words, but with deep recognition — and then fades into mist. You now hold the book, the staff, and the flame. You are the bard.

Sacred Reflection

How can I express my truth as a poet, author, musician or singer? Words and sound carry spells. This question helps you explore your role as a sacred voice: a bridge between unseen worlds and human hearts through artistic language.

Ritual

Lyric, Book, and Flame

Supplies
- A blue or gold candle (for truth or inspiration)
- An object of inspiration (e.g., photo, lyric, poem, or relic)
- A journal and pen
- Incense or essential oil (lavender, sandalwood, or clove)
- A creative medium (e.g., instrument, paint, clay, or your voice)

Step 1: Create the Sacred Space.

Begin at twilight or dawn, when the veil between worlds is soft. Light incense, and place The Bard oracle card at the center of your altar or workspace. Carefully arrange your tools around it. Light a candle to awaken your inner flame, and close your eyes.

Place one hand on your throat chakra and the other on your heart. Breathe in through your nose and out through your mouth three times. With each breath, draw in inspiration and exhale doubt. Visualize standing barefoot in the dewy grass beside the cloaked elder. The triskelion spins above you, and the amber crystal glows within.

Step 2: Invocation – Call the Bardic Flame.

Speak, sing, write, or play your invocation aloud. Use whatever form stirs your soul. Speak this suggested invocation:
"Muse of memory, spirit of song,
Ancestors of story and spell —
Move through me now.
Let what needs to be told
Rise from my soul
And travel with me through the lands.
I am the vessel. The bard walks beside me."

Step 3: Embody the Triskelion – Activate Body, Mind, Spirit.

Sit with an object of inspiration and ask, *"What wishes to be expressed through me today?"* Let your body (hands), mind (thoughts), and spirit (intuition) collaborate. Journal, sing, paint, dance, or sculpt. Do not judge; channel what arises.

You are not just making art — you are crafting living memory from what you have seen, survived, loved, and learned. This is how the bard turns experience into legacy.

Step 4: Speak the Spell – Declare Your Truth.

When your creation feels complete, place it on the altar. Say aloud, *"This is my truth. This is my song. This is my magic to share."* Feel its vibration in your chest. You have honored the bard within.

Step 5: Offer to the Echo – Share or Preserve.

Leave your creation on the altar for at least one day. You may share it or keep it as a sacred seed. Optional: Anoint it or place a crystal beside it.

Step 6: Express Gratitude and Release.

Blow out the candle. Thank the muse, the triskelion, and any guides who moved through you. Speak or write your gratitude.

Step 7: Return to the Flame – Integrate.

Carry your voice into the world. Wear blue or gold. Hum your melody. Revisit your journal in a week. This ritual is not a moment — it is a thread in your becoming.

Speak this closing affirmation: *"I am the bard. I remember. I create. I rise. I sing the world into being."*

Essence

Autonomy

Self-Trust

Sanctum

Sacred Rite

Wild Wisdom

Authenticity

Dragonfly Echo

I am the keeper of my own flame and cauldron. My solitude is my sanctuary. My magic is my own, and it is mighty. I stand in my power and follow my soul's goal. I trust myself with the energy I invoke and the powerful vibration I become.

9. Solitary Practitioner

Energetic Invitation: This card arrives to affirm your sacred independence and intuitive path. As a solitary practitioner, your power is not diminished by standing alone — it is defined by it. You walk the path of autonomy, where decisions are rooted in self-trust, not external validation. You embody the mystic who listens deeply, the dreamer who dances with silence, and the ritualist whose altar is the earth itself.

Your spiritual practice is not shaped by doctrine, but by devotion. You stir your cauldron with intention, tend your flame with care, and blend crystals and herbs as allies in your sacred rites. You require no witness or approval. Your magic is born of presence and powered by your personal truth. You create from your sanctum, a private temple woven from instinct and imagination.

This is the realm of wild wisdom, where teachings rise from dreams, nature, and ancestral knowing. You are the weaver of paths, not the follower. You walk barefoot between realms with reverence and clarity. You are your own lineage, your own temple, and your own teacher.

This card reminds you: You do not need a coven, mentor, or structured tradition to be whole. You are the flame and the keeper, the question and the answer. Your authenticity is your ritual. Your solitude is not absence — it is sacred space.

You are the spell. You are sovereign. You are self-initiated. Walk proudly in your light. The path of the solitary is ancient and holy — quiet, yes, but never alone. Spirit walks beside you.

Autonomy • Self-Trust • Sanctum • Sacred Rite • Wild Wisdom • Authenticity

Solitary Practitioner

6

Shadow Path

The shadow path of the solitary practitioner can arise as isolation, rigidity, or spiritual superiority. In your pursuit of independence, you may unintentionally build walls instead of boundaries, mistaking solitude for separation. Autonomy becomes avoidance when it shields you from vulnerability or meaningful connection.

You may struggle to trust others, which can lead to spiritual pride or the illusion that your way is the only way. You may also silence your own needs for support, forgetting that sovereignty does not mean going it alone.

The work lies in opening space for shared wisdom without sacrificing self-trust. Honor your sanctum; let the winds of others' insights pass through now and then. Even in solitude, there is room for resonance, reflection, and remembering connection is also sacred.

Symbolic Vision: Under the velvet glow of the full moon, a solitary witch stands within her sanctum — a sacred space woven of shadow, flame, and breath. Her hair glows like platinum flame, flickering in rhythm with the fire at her feet.

Before her, a cauldron bubbles with enchanted brew. Wildflowers, herbs, and oils spill from her palm in quiet devotion, igniting the rising smoke into spell-threaded wisps. These spirals carry her intention upward, weaving prayers into the night air.

Behind her, ancient standing stones rise — sentinels of magic lore, echoing with the silent truths of time. Their presence speaks to the wild wisdom of those who came before, rites whispered under stars, and secrets held in stone. The wind moves through the

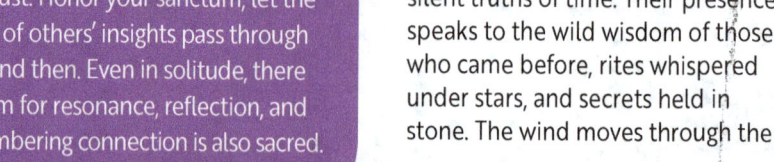

Salisbury Plain, rustling grasses like sacred breath, wrapping her in the voices of ancestors and the rhythm of the land. Each movement she makes is deliberate. Each word spoken is an incantation, a vow, and a sacred rite.

Her spells are not born solely of recipe but also of self-trust, intention, and memory. She does not brew for spectacle; she brews because it is who she is. She is the witch and the wand. She is the grimoire and the guardian. Each blend she stirs, each breath she takes, each whisper of desire and devotion — these are her spells.

She walks alone, but never without power. Hers is a path of authenticity, not performance. A journey led by autonomy, not permission. She is both seeker and priestess, barefoot on the moss and crowned in starlight. The solitary practitioner is the wild mystic who has chosen her own sacred rhythm — the hedge witch, dream weaver, or the one who listens to nature and follows her own inner drum. She does not need a circle to find her magic. Her sanctum is within. Her craft is her communion. Her life is a ritual.

She listens to owls, follows moon tides, and remembers spells spoken by firelight and seafoam. She is not bound by temple walls or external scripts. Her magic is alive and ancestral, forged in the fire of authentic self-knowing. The priestess at Stonehenge rises in her as an ancient echo of spiritual independence and timeless knowing.

This card is a mirror to your sacred independence — a reminder that solitude is not lack but strength, and not isolation but alignment. It is the sanctuary where your true voice is heard and your deepest power blooms.

You do not need a coven to be powerful. You do not need permission to be magical. You are the spell. You are the sacred rite. Your path — rooted in devotion, wild wisdom, and soul truth — is more than enough.

Sacred Reflection

In what ways do I create sacred space for myself, and how can I strengthen it as my sanctuary? Write into the physical and energetic spaces that support your rituals. What could be enhanced to more deeply honor your path?

Ritual

Solitary Practitioner Brew

Supplies

- A heat-safe cauldron or pot (preferably cast iron, copper, or ceramic)
- A wooden spoon or ritual stirring tool
- Fresh or dried herbs
- Essential oils that align to your intention: rose, lavender, or hibiscus for love and self-worth; mugwort, rosemary, or black pepper for protection and banishing; basil, cinnamon, or bay leaf for abundance and success; sage, mint, or lemon balm for intuition and clarity
- A journal and pen
- A candle (black for banishing, white for purity, red for passion, green for abundance)
- Crystals of your choice (optional)

Step 1: Cast the Circle of Self.

Use salt, herbs, leaves, flour, or whatever you resonate with to create a circle around you. Light your candle and breathe deeply. Declare aloud, *"I call this space sacred. I stand alone although never without power. This circle is cast in my name and nature."*

Take three deep breaths. As you inhale, call energy into your core. As you exhale, release distraction. Feel your feet grounded, your heart present, and your spirit centered.

Step 2: Define Your Intention.

In your journal, write a one-line spell or desire (e.g., *"I call abundance into my path"* or *"I release fear and rise in truth"*). Whisper it three times, feeding it with breath from deep in your belly. Visualize beams of light transmitting this desire from your body to the universe. This is the soul of your brew.

Step 3: Select and Bless the Herbs

Choose three to five herbs or oils that match your intention. Hold each one and say, *"I awaken your spirit and call your power to my purpose."* Let your wild wisdom choose intuitively. Feel each plant stir under your touch.

Step 4: Kindle the Flame.

Prepare a pot or cauldron with water and gentle heat. Begin stirring with a rhythm that matches your energy. Say, *"As fire awakens water, so my will awakens this spell."*

Step 5: Add the Herbs with Intention.

One by one, add your chosen ingredients into the simmering water. With each addition, stir clockwise and repeat your spell. Let the scent rise like sacred incense. This is a living ritual. The brew is listening.

Step 6: Breathe the Spell into Being.

Hover your hands over the pot. Close your eyes. Stir with your dominant hand and say, *"This brew is charged. This spell is stirred by herb and heat, breath and word."* Stand in silence. Feel the energy of the potion meet your own. This is spellwork through presence — raw and real.

Step 7: Seal and Send the Energy.

Turn off the heat. When cool, strain the liquid. You may anoint yourself or your tools, pour at your threshold, use it in candle magick, or return it to the earth in gratitude.

Speak these closing words, *"This spell is brewed; my will is true. What's done in steam now flows through you."* Your sanctum holds the spell. You are the rite.

10. Runes

Essence
Divine Language
Sacred Codes
Prophetic Whispers
Archetypes

Dragonfly Echo

I am open to receiving guidance from the unseen ancient realms. My path is shaped by sigils. I trust the sacred language of Spirit to illuminate my way, whispering truths that awaken the soul. I honor the runes as sacred tools, used for divination and ritual, woven through time and Spirit.

Energetic Invitation: The Runes card is an invitation to commune with a divine language — a sacred, symbolic dialect shaped by ancient hands and cosmic time. These sacred codes carry keys to intuition, destiny, and soul wisdom.

Each rune is a living archetype — a fragment of myth aligned with the rhythms of earth and sky. Truth is not always spoken; sometimes it is etched in symbol, carved in stone, or whispered through dreams. The runes speak through the subtle stones, sigils, omens, and echoes. They ask for reverence, not analysis.

You are being called to symbolic perception and to attune your awareness to the voice of the unseen. Repeating numbers, animal messengers, flickering lights, and meaningful songs are also runes as modern reflections of an ancient tongue. They are echoes of the stones and the wisdom of the ancestors.

This is a return to divine language, a way of listening beyond words and understanding the soul's conversation with the cosmos. The runes are sacred codes, imprinted with frequencies that awaken inner knowing and unlock intuitive insight.

You are not solving a puzzle; you are receiving archetypal guidance. These symbols activate remembrance, not instruction. Their power lives in presence and deep listening.

Through sacrifice and revelation, the veils part. What must be surrendered is certainty. What is revealed is deeper truth. Trust what you feel. The runes are already speaking within and around you. Can you see their language?

Shadow Path

The Runes card reversed may signal a disconnection from your intuitive voice or a reluctance to listen to signs. You may be caught in the grip of overanalysis, dismissing the synchronicities, patterns, and whispers that once guided you. The sacred symbols are still there, but perhaps you have forgotten how to see.

This reversal invites you to reawaken your symbolic literacy and reclaim your ability to perceive meaning beyond logic. The language of the soul cannot be deciphered by intellect alone.

You are being nudged to slow down and attune once more to the divine language woven into your days. Return to ritual. Return to signs. Return to the ancient sources. The universe is a mirror, and it is always speaking. The question is, Are you still listening?

Symbolic Vision: Runes have been cast upon the altar, scattered like whispers from the unseen across a glowing emerald cloth. This sacred green square radiates with earth magic, bordered in intricate light, and rests atop a golden table of energy — a sun-soaked threshold between realms. The energy surrounding the table hums with warmth, echoing the pulse of ancient fire and ancestral guidance.

At the center of the altar is a powerful symbol: the triquetra, or trinity knot, painted radiant purple. This ancient Celtic sigil, composed of three interlaced arcs enclosed within a circle, holds deep esoteric resonance. It represents the eternal unity of life cycles — birth, death, and rebirth — as well as the interwoven dance of body, mind, and soul. The circle that encloses it is a symbol of divine wholeness and protection, anchoring the runework in sacred intention.

Each rune placed around the triquetra carries a magnetic stillness, as if mid-whisper. These are not just symbols; they are living keys, carved from stone and time, designed to unlock intuition, awaken archetypal truths, and reconnect you to the divine language of the cosmos.

The golden glow of the table beneath reflects the wisdom of the sun and the inner fire of revelation. You are not merely observing this layout — you are being invited to stand within it. This is a call to listen, receive, and remember the sacred codes etched across your own timeline. This card is an opening — a mirror, a map, a message. Let the runes speak.

Each rune in the Elder Futhark is a living current of myth, memory, and magic — a sacred sigil echoing the language of spirit. Divided into three rune families called *aettir*, these symbols guide the soul through birth, challenge, and return.

Fehu ignites abundance and creative flow, while Uruz awakens raw strength and becoming. Thurisaz disrupts illusions with protective force, and Ansuz carries divine speech and ancestral breath. Raidho marks the soul's journey, and Kenaz lights the inner fire of revelation. Gebo blesses sacred exchange; Wunjo sings of joy and soul harmony. Hagalaz storms through stagnation, and Nauthiz births purpose through tension. Isa calls for stillness, Jera rewards patience.

Eihwaz is the yew of endurance and rebirth; Perthro unveils mystery and fate. Algiz shields with sacred guidance, while Sowilo brings radiance and victory. Tiwaz invokes justice and sacrifice; Berkano nurtures birth and renewal. Ehwaz moves in trust and alignment; Mannaz reflects the shared mirror of humanity. Laguz flows with intuition and dream; Ingwaz holds the fertile seed within. Dagaz delivers breakthrough and awakening, and Othala grounds us in legacy and soul roots.

Together, these runes form a divine map — each a key and whisper of the sacred woven into time.

Sacred Reflection

Which rune or archetype feels most alive in my field right now, and what part of me is it calling forth? Tune into your inner landscape. What rune mirrors your current path, challenge, or potential? Let it speak through story, sensation, or memory.

Ritual

Crafting a Rune Stone

- A natural stone, piece of wood, or clay disk (palm-sized)
- A rune symbol that calls to you (from the Elder Futhark or one that resonates)
- Carving tool (woodburning pen, engraving tool, or sharp stylus) or fine paintbrush and acrylic paint
- A cloth or casting surface (altar cloth, fur, moss, or bark)
- Anointing oil (mugwort, frankincense, or a wild-crafted sacred blend)
- Candle (white for purity, black for shadow work, green for growth or earth-based runes)
- Journal
- Optional: herbs such as yarrow, vervain, or juniper to sprinkle during consecration

Step 1: Prepare Your Sacred Space.

Attune yourself to the ancient runic language through presence and intention. This ritual is not simply a craft; it is a sacred act of devotion. You are entering into a dialogue between seeker and symbol, body and spirit, earth and ether.

Cleanse your space using smoke, bells, or salt-infused water charged with herbs. Lay your casting cloth, moss, or sacred surface before you. Light your chosen candle, and pause to feel the shift in the energy. Say aloud, *"I open the veil between worlds. May this space be sacred, protected, and alive with magic."* Let the atmosphere settle. Know that you have opened a portal of connection.

Step 2: Choose the Rune That Chooses You.

Slowly review the list of runes. Gently hold your blank stone, wood, or clay disk in your hands. Close your eyes and whisper, *"What symbol does my soul carry today?"* Let the answer rise through sensation — perhaps as an image, word, heat, or inner knowing. If you feel uncertain, meditate with the Elder Futhark chart, and notice which symbol speaks to you from beyond logic.

Step 3: Carve, Paint or Draw with Devotion.

Using your carving or painting tools, begin inscribing the chosen rune onto your object. Chant or intone the rune's name as you work. Let each stroke be filled with presence. Carve or paint slowly, allowing the spirit of the rune to infuse the material. This is a merging of essence and symbol. Feel the power of the rune anchoring through your hands into the world of form.

Step 4: Anoint and Consecrate.

Anoint your rune with sacred oil — mugwort, frankincense, or a blend that calls to your spirit. Surround it with herbs such as yarrow, vervain, or juniper. Hold the rune to your heart and declare, *"By the flame of the gods, by the bones of the earth, by the whisper of the ancestors, I consecrate this rune."*

Step 5: Charge with Flame.

Gently hover the rune over the candle's flame without burning it. Let the warmth seep into the rune. Visualize it glowing with ancient fire and pulsing with remembered power.

Step 6: Awaken and Listen.

Place your rune on the cloth. Sit with it. Breathe. Journal the messages or symbols that arise. Ask yourself,
· What is this rune teaching me?
· What phase of life is it illuminating?
· What must I embody to walk with its power?

Step 7: Close the Ritual.

Offer gratitude to the spirits, guides, and ancestors who have witnessed this act. Extinguish the candle. Place your rune in a pouch, box, or sacred space. You may continue to craft more stones as you are guided, or work with this one as a living talisman, teacher, and ally.

II. Pandora's Box

Essence

Forbidden Curiosity

Chaos and Catalyst

Truth and Sorrow

Unleashing Potential

Dragonfly Echo

I honor the wisdom in curiosity and trust my inner voice to guide me through the unknown. Even disobedience, when led by soul, can reveal hidden truths and sacred transformation. My path is shaped by symbols and shadows, and I do not fear what lies beneath. Pain may be released, although hope remains as a beacon of possibility amid darkness even through the tempest.

Energetic Invitation: Temptation is rising. Something in your life or psyche is calling you to peer beneath the surface — into something hidden, mysterious, or even forbidden.

This card carries the energy of forbidden curiosity, the pull toward what has been locked away for too long. Will your hunger for truth lead to sorrow or to the unleashing of potential long buried?

Pandora's Box is a mythic mirror reflecting your relationship with risk, trust, and sacred desire. The ancient story is that Pandora, whose name means "all-gifted," was given a sealed jar and told not to open it. But curiosity stirred within her — deep, instinctual, and unstoppable. She opened it, and from that moment chaos was released. Pain, fear, suffering, and grief flew out into the world. But one thing remained: hope.

This card is not a warning — it is an initiation. You are being asked to examine your motives. Are you chasing shadow for sensation or honoring shadow as a path to transformation? Chaos can be a catalyst, and the box that contains pain may also contain prophecy.

This moment is about choices made at the threshold. You become responsible for what you open. Truth may be entangled with sorrow, but it is also the way home.

Approach the mystery with reverence. Let your courage be tempered with awareness. The box is not a curse — it is a key.

Forbidden Curiosity • Chaos and Catalyst • Unleashing Potential
Truth and Sorrow •

Pandora's Box

II

Shadow Path

Pandora's Box reversed may signal reckless curiosity, impulsive choices, or resistance to facing uncomfortable truths. You may be chasing sensation without grounding or avoiding the deeper inner work your soul is calling for. Denial can become its own sealed box, locking you away from the wisdom your shadows carry.

There is a difference between exploration and escapism. Are you opening doors out of alignment or refusing to open them at all?

Curiosity has power. Honor it with awareness. What you open may not be undone, but what it reveals may set you free. Transformation cannot happen without truth. If fear has held you back, let courage now take its place. The mystery remains, but it awaits your conscious and reverent engagement.

Symbolic Vision: A red-haired woman kneels before an ornate, stained-glass box, its edges etched with divine patterns and secrets long hidden. The box pulses with otherworldly energy, its surface glowing like the embers of a forgotten star. Her hand  has already lifted the lid. What was sealed is now released.

From its shimmering seams, shadow spills forth. A swirl of winged beings — bats, smoke-serpents, and a stone gargoyle — emerge like ancient protectors and spectral warnings. The gargoyle crouches with haunting stillness, eyes lit by the memory of guardianship. The bats twist midair as messengers of the liminal, casting flickers of fate.

The smoke that follows is not passive; it is charged with emotion, ancestral memory, and unseen knowing. Each tendril dances like prophecy, encircling the seeker in riddles yet to be named.

Above her, a vision forms. The image of the goddess rises from the mist, radiant from within. Her halo spreads in all directions — a flare of celestial light cutting through the chaos. She is not separate from the box; she is born of it, transcendent and whole. Her presence is protective, not punishing, holding within her gaze the silent vow of hope.

The bench where the woman kneels bears the triple moon symbol of feminine power — the spiral womb of creation, destruction, and return. Her hands tremble, not in fear, but in sacred curiosity. She is not frozen; she is listening. She is choosing. This is not simply chaos. It is choice.

In Greek myth, Pandora's tale has long been misunderstood. The "box" was never a box, but a sacred jar — *pithos*, an earthen vessel of initiation. Pandora, meaning "all-gifted," was the first woman formed by the gods, blessed with grace, beauty, voice, and deep curiosity. Her opening of the jar was not foolishness — it was a descent into awareness.

Though shadow and sorrow were released, hope remained. It lingered, not trapped, but waiting, hovering like a distant star above the veil.

This myth was not crafted to shame feminine desire. It was meant to reveal its power. Forbidden curiosity becomes transformation when met with courage. Chaos is the catalyst. The box may open sorrow, but it also opens prophecy. Within it lie truth and sorrow but also the unleashing of potential.

To question the rules, to follow your inner ache, even when it disrupts everything, is also sacred.

You are this seeker. You are the trembling hand on the box of your own becoming. Will you open it?

Sacred Reflection

What am I secretly curious about — an idea, desire, or truth I have hesitated to explore? Does it feel forbidden because of others' expectations or your own self-doubt? Where in your life is curiosity tugging at your spirit, asking to be honored?

Ritual

Sacred Curiosity and Catalyst

Supplies

- A box or jar (ornate, wooden, glass, or hand-decorated)
- 2 candles (black and white or red and gold)
- A truth crystal (obsidian, clear quartz, or labradorite)
- A feather, shell, or star charm (your "hope" token)
- Strips of paper and a pen
- A fire-safe bowl or cauldron
- Optional: essential oil or anointing blend (mugwort, frankincense, rose)

Step 1: Cast the Sacred Circle.

Light both candles, and place the box or jar at the center of your ritual space. Breathe deeply. Whisper, *"This space is sacred. This moment is mine."* Cleanse with smoke or sound. Feel the veil thin as you center yourself between worlds.

Step 2: Anoint and Activate the Vessel.

Touch the box with care and reverence. Dab it with oil, if called. Say, *"You are the mirror of mystery. You hold the sorrow, the shadow, and the spark."*

Step 3: Call the Myth into Presence.

Speak aloud or whisper, *"I call upon Pandora, the all-gifted. I summon the myth and the memory. May what is ready to be seen rise from shadow into knowing."*

Step 4: **Write Down the Shadow and the Catalyst.**

On the first strip of paper, write something you have denied — what's been feared, suppressed, or called "too much."

On the second strip, write the truth or longing that has pulled at your soul. What has tempted your curiosity?

Fold both pieces of paper, and place them in the box or jar.

Step 5: **Stir the Chaos.**

Gently shake the box or jar or swirl its contents. Let emotion rise. Say, *"Within this vessel is not just danger. There is initiation."* Feel the tension between fear and hunger. Let it build.

Step 6: **Open the Box or Jar, and Burn the Lies.**

With reverence, open the box or jar. Gaze into it. Read each slip of paper aloud. Burn each one in your bowl, releasing them into smoke.

Say, *"From chaos comes clarity. From truth, transformation."* Let the fire be your witness.

Step 7: **Seal the Box or Jar with Hope and Truth.**

Place your charm (feather, shell, or star) into the now-empty box or jar. Say, *"Even in the unraveling, I plant the seed of hope."*

Hold your crystal. Breathe. Let truth settle in your body. Declare, *"I am the hinge between shadow and salvation. I am not reckless; I am ready. I choose curiosity. I choose awakening."*

Close the lid, and whisper, *"This is no longer a curse. It is my sacred mirror."*

12. Spiritus Mundi

Energetic Invitation: You are tapping into a force older than time and vaster than space. Spiritus Mundi, Latin for "world soul," is the shared breath of the collective soul — a cosmic weave of memory, myth, archetype, and ancient knowing. It is the living field of Akashic awareness, the soul stream where every story, symbol, and spirit resides beyond time.

When this card appears, you are not imagining; you are remembering. Dreams, visions, intuitive flashes, and soul whispers may arrive swiftly. They are not coincidence. You are tuning into cosmic intelligence, a vibrational stream that speaks through symbols, synchronicities, and quiet revelations.

This is the hum of quantum energy pulsing across timelines, dimensions, and destinies. You are walking the dragline of consciousness, tracing connections between stars and cells, ancestors and oracles, past and possibility. What stirs in you now does not belong to you alone. It belongs to the greater unfolding. You are becoming a vessel through which Spiritus Mundi breathes. Divine inspiration is activating and emerging from within you, encoded in your soul's memory. The past whispers. The future hums. The now opens. You are the bridge between what was and what is becoming.

As you awaken, you amplify. The vibration you hold contributes to the planetary resonance. Your remembrance strengthens the signal of the world soul. You are not just receiving the transmission; you are becoming part of it. Remember your place in the tapestry. The world soul is speaking through you.

Essence

Collective Soul
Akashic Awareness
Divine Inspiration
Cosmic Intelligence
Quantum Energy

Dragonfly Echo

You are connected to the great spider web of consciousness. Your soul is a thread in the infinite tapestry of creation. What flows through me is not mine alone; it is the voice of stars, ancestors, and Source. You are electric. You follow the silver thread of Spiritus Mundi, the dragline of the soul, woven through myth, memory, and dream.

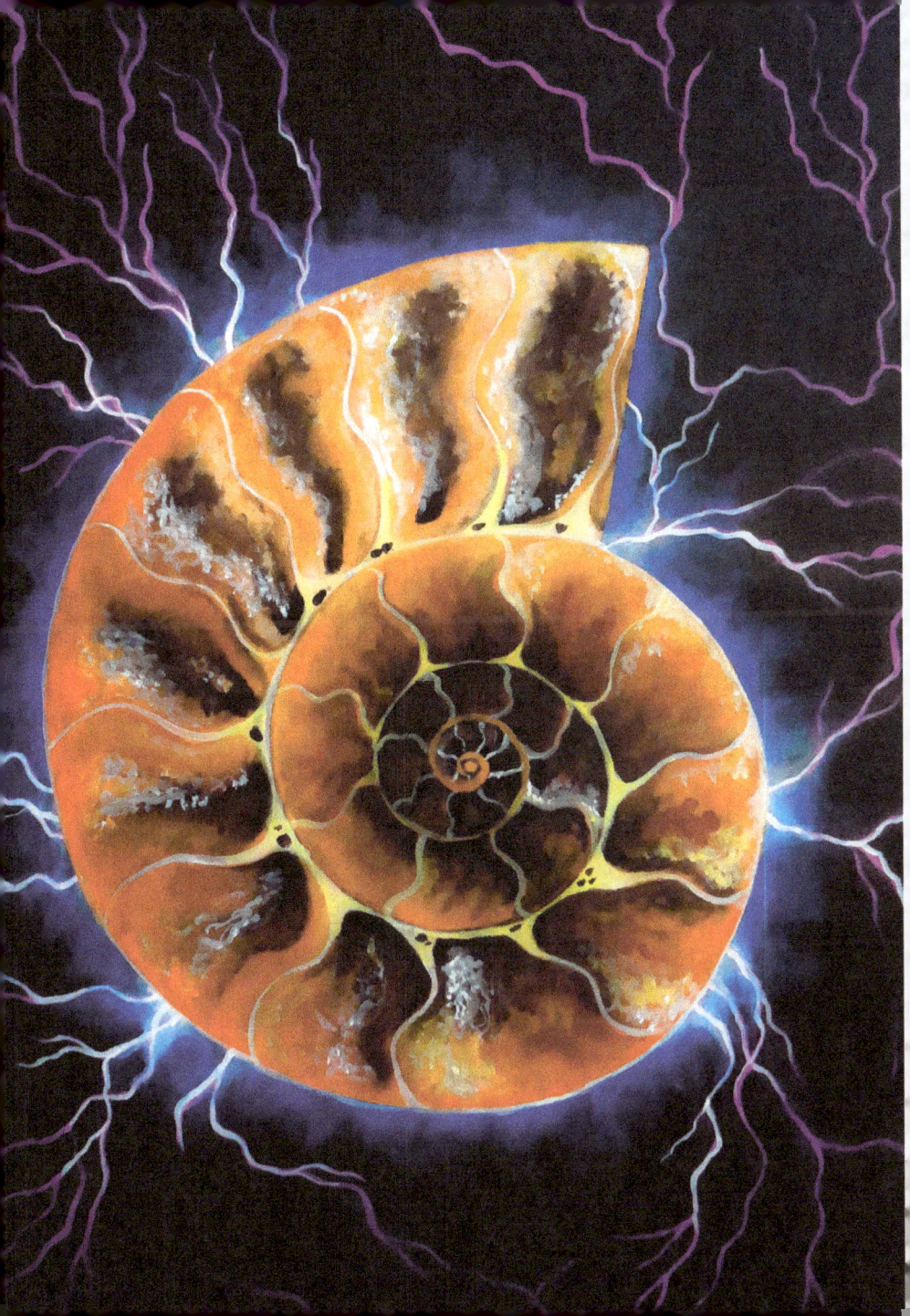

Spiritus Mundi

12

Cosmic Intelligence • Quantum Energy
Collective Soul • Akashic Awareness • Divine Inspiration

Shadow Path

When reversed, Spiritus Mundi may reflect spiritual static, energetic overwhelm, or a loss of attunement to your inner voice. You may be over-relying on logic or ego while silencing the subtle threads of intuition. This disconnection from cosmic intelligence creates noise, confusion, or creative block. You are still held within the collective soul, but your channel may be clouded.

There is no punishment here, only invitation. Step back. Breathe. Akashic awareness is not something you force; it is something you feel. Quantum energy moves through stillness. Divine inspiration flows from surrender.

Your sacred remembering is waiting beneath the chaos. Realign. Unplug. The world soul has not gone silent — you've simply lost the signal. Listen again. The transmission is still singing.

Symbolic Vision: A glowing ammonite spiral unfurls at the center of the vision — its chambers illuminated from within like a sacred scroll curled into the shape of time itself. This is no ordinary fossil. It is a living symbol of memory, patterned with the golden spiral — the divine ratio that governs not just physical form but also the sacred geometry of the soul's evolution across time, timelines, and dimensions.

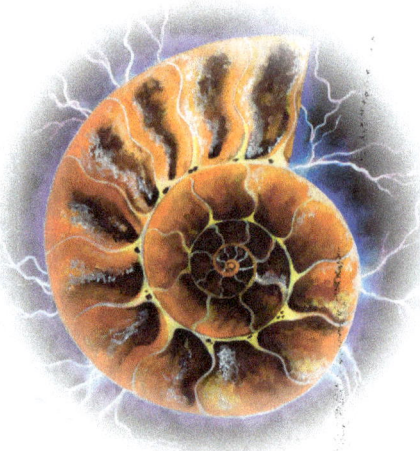

The spiral becomes a portal, alive with vibration and light. Each chamber hums with the resonance of memory and possibility. Within its form lies a soul record: a living map of past lives, lineage, and latent gifts. This is not static history; it is a breathing archive of the collective soul, turning within you like a celestial gear.

Across the horizon, a strike of lightning illuminates the darkened field — not as destruction, but as activation. It moves like synaptic fire through space, awakening insight and linking form with formless. This is the current of cosmic intelligence, alive within the ether, connecting thought to truth in an instant. You are not just witnessing it — you are participating in it.

This is the frequency of quantum energy: the ever-present pulse that flows through all creation and perception. It does not wait for belief; it moves through coherence and is felt as instinct, knowing, or revelation.

The spiral holds the resonance of Akashic awareness. You do not decode this library — you remember it. Its language is vibration, imagery, symbol, and sensation. You have read it before in dreams, visions, or the deep stillness beneath the noise.

Divine inspiration pours from the center like breath, reaching into your creative essence. It is not something you call — it is something you recognize. This energy is what speaks through poets, prophets, artists, and mystics who remember that they are not alone.

This is the spirit behind the symbol. It is the song within the silence.

Poet W.B. Yeats described Spiritus Mundi as the realm from which all symbols, archetypes, and insight arise — a collective consciousness that connects all beings and fuels the imagination. He believed this dimension shaped his poetry and gave voice to his visions of history, humanity, and spiritual truth. It was not inspiration alone — it was communion.

You are both the spiral and the spark. You are the one who listens, the one who speaks, and the one who remembers.

Let it move through your hands, your thoughts, and your craft.

You are not separate from source. You are Spiritus Mundi made form.

Sacred Reflection

When do I feel most connected to divine intelligence or universal flow? Reflect on what allows you to open effortlessly to higher guidance. What sensations, symbols, or knowing arises when you are fully attuned to something greater than yourself?

Ritual

Spiral of Soul Memory

Supplies

- An ammonite fossil or spiral-shaped object or drawing
- A white candle
- Herbs (mugwort, lavender, or frankincense)
- Journal or parchment and a pen
- Optional: drawing or print of the Fibonacci spiral or sacred geometry

Step 1: Prepare the Space.

Create a quiet sanctum where you will not be disturbed. Place an ammonite fossil or spiral-shaped object at the center of your altar. Light a white candle to symbolize pure consciousness and burn herbs like mugwort, lavender, or frankincense to open intuitive channels. Optionally, place a drawing or print of the Fibonacci spiral or sacred geometry nearby.

Step 2: Ground in the Body, Expand the Field.

Sit or stand with your spine aligned. Close your eyes and begin slow, conscious breathing. With each inhale, imagine drawing energy from the Earth's core into your root. With each exhale, imagine sending your breath into the stars. After several rounds, feel yourself centered between Earth and cosmos with your body a bridge and your breath a prayer.

Step 3: Activate the Spiral.

Hold the ammonite or place your hands above the image of the spiral. Slowly trace the spiral inward with your finger or mind's eye. As you move toward the center, silently repeat, *"I return to the source. I remember what is mine."* Pause in stillness at the center, imagining light gathering there. Then trace outward while saying, *"I carry the light forward. I embody what is divine."*

Step 4: Invoke the Lightning.

Visualize bolts of lightning streaming into your crown and down your spine, activating your inner channels. Say aloud or whisper, *"Sacred current of cosmic fire, awaken in me. Transmitter of truth, electrify my soul. Let me receive the wisdom of the ages. Let me become a vessel of divine intelligence."* Feel the tingling sensation in your body as this quantum energy flows through you.

Step 5: Scribe the Message.

Take a journal or parchment and begin free writing. Don't filter. This is a direct channeling of divine inspiration. Ask, *"What message does the collective soul want me to know? What symbols, images, or truths am I being shown?"* Let your hand become the conduit for the spiral's language.

Step 6: Speak into the Field.

Read aloud what you wrote as a spoken declaration. Offer it to the universe. If working with sound, you may tone a vowel (such as "Ah" or "Om") to vibrate your words into the quantum field. Imagine your voice weaving into the spiral of consciousness, co-creating with Spirit.

Step 7: Seal the Spiral.

Bring your palms together at your heart. Offer gratitude to the ammonite, the lightning, the ancients, and unseen intelligence you have touched. Whisper, *"I am the breath of Spirit made form. I am the oracle. I am the Mundi."* Blow out the candle, and sit in silence for several minutes, letting the resonance settle. Close the ritual by touching earth, body, and sky — anchoring the spiral within.

13. Goddess Hekate

Energetic Invitation: Goddess Hekate, ancient guardian of thresholds and deep mysteries, walks beside those at the edge of becoming. She is the triple goddess of transition, magick, and inner knowing — torchbearer of the unseen. With one foot in the realm of the living and the other in shadow, she stands at the crossroads, where choices shape destiny. When this card appears, it is a sacred summons. You are being asked to step into your power, choose courage over comfort, and claim the keys that have always been yours.

Hekate honors boundaries not as walls, but as sacred markings — lines of initiation and protection. She teaches that resistance is not the enemy, but the gatekeeper to change. Her serpents coil with ancient memory, whispering truths from beneath the surface. She is the weaver of soul threads, crafting transformation through ritual and dream.

With origins in Anatolia and later venerated in Greek and Roman traditions, Hekate is the embodiment of prophecy, protection, and liminality. Her essence flows through other cultural expressions, such as the Morrigan and Cailleach.

Her torches light the way through inner dark, revealing not fear, but freedom. Her black dogs guard the path as loyal sentinels of the soul's journey. Her presence asks not for blind faith, but for brave remembrance.

You do not need a map — you are the map and the spell. Hekate walks with you, her fire illuminating every step toward sacred becoming. The crossroads are open. Will you step through?

Essence
Magick
Transition
Keys
Resistance
Crossroads
Boundaries

Dragonfly Echo

I walk the crossroads with courage. I hold the key to my becoming. Hekate walks with me in shadow, in silence, and in sovereignty. I am a vessel of powerful magick, and my path is lit with enchanted purpose.

Goddess Hekate

Shadow Path

When Hekate appears reversed, it signals fear of change, resistance to inner transformation, or hesitation at a crucial threshold. You may be clinging to the familiar, doubting your intuitive knowing, or avoiding the initiation that beckons.

This card suggests you are stuck between worlds — aware of what must shift but unwilling to act. The crossroads are before you, yet your inner fire flickers with uncertainty. Her sacred tools — keys, torches, and serpents — remain dormant when ignored. Reversed, Hekate warns of fragmented energy, avoidance of shadow work, and a refusal to honor your own magick.

This is a sacred pause. Trust your inner flame. Even in the dark, your soul knows the way. The keys are still in your hand. Will you claim them?

Symbolic Vision: Hekate stands at the luminous crossroads, veiled in twilight and woven in shadow. She is both guardian and guide of liminal spaces — the sacred thresholds between worlds, identities, and initiations. Her triple form represents the eternal spiral of time: past, present, and future. She holds dominion over what is ending, what is rising, and what has yet to be named. Her power lives in moments of decision, in portals not yet opened, and in the fierce stillness before transformation.

Winding around her arms and waist is the serpent — a symbol of sacred knowledge, eternal renewal, and the mysteries that sleep beneath the surface of all things. This is not a creature of fear but of ancient wisdom, reminding us that all change requires a shedding. Hekate teaches that to claim the next version of yourself, you must release what no longer carries your truth.

Her crown bears the triskele, the triple-spiral glyph of sacred motion. It pulses with the energy of transition, marking her as a timeless traveler through the cycles of death, birth, and rebirth. She wears a key, gleaming with purpose. This is no ordinary key; it grants access to the unseen, the inner realms, and the deeper knowing you already carry. It is the symbol of sovereignty, discernment, and power claimed.

In her hands are twin torches, blazing with the fire of magick. These torches light the path forward when logic fails. They burn away illusion, fear, and distraction. They are the sacred fire that reveals the way through the shadow and out of confusion. They illuminate the crossroads, that sacred point of choice where destiny is shaped by courage.

Two black dogs rest at her feet, wtih their gaze unwavering. These are not passive animals — they are companions of the underworld, gatekeepers of intuition, and guardians of thresholds. They walk with those willing to face shadow and listen to its teachings. They do not flinch from the unknown; they guide us into it.

Beneath her feet, the dagger rests. It is the tool of boundaries and of cutting cords, illusions, and old oaths. It is the sacred weapon of clarity. Wielded with care, it defends your becoming.

The presence of Hekate is a revelation of resistance — not as refusal, but as sacred preservation. She is the still voice when noise surrounds you. She is the crossroads. She does not tell you which path to take — she reminds you that the choice is yours, and you already hold the keys.

Sacred Reflection

What does magick mean to me when no one is watching, and how do I embody it through presence, practice, or wordless knowing? Where in your life are you being asked to reclaim your magick — not as performance, but as power?

Ritual
The Crossroads Flame

Supplies

- *Two candles (traditionally black or white to represent torches)*
- *An athame or ritual dagger*
- *A key (physical or symbolic)*
- *Flour, chalk, or spray paint to draw or mark a crossroads*
- *A representation of black dogs (figurines, photos, or talismans)*
- *A symbol or statue of a snake (or a coiled cord, drawing, or charm)*
- *Optional: incense, cloak, stones to mark corners of the ritual space*

Step 1: Prepare the Crossroads.

Whether outside or indoors, draw or mark a crossroads on the ground using chalk, flour, or spray paint — marking a large equal-armed "X" within your ritual space. This becomes your portal of transition. Place the two candles at opposing ends of the crossroads to represent Hekate's flaming torches. These flames serve as guardians of sacred passage and protection.

Step 2: Call the Guardians.

Place your dog representations at two quadrants of the crossroads, and the snake symbol in another. These are your sentinels. Say, *"By fang and coil, by flame and gate, guardians of the veil, I ask you wait. Protect this rite, stand in-between — through shadow and light, be still, unseen."*

Step 3: Cast the Circle of Resistance.

Take your athame or dagger, and walk clockwise around the space, visualizing boundaries being drawn with each step. As you walk say, *"By this blade, I draw the line. All that is not of will, remain outside. This is my circle of resistance and power — Here I stand at the edge of the hour."*

Step 4: Light the Torches of Transition.

Light the two candles, and place the key at the center of the crossroads. Say, *"Flames of Hekate, blaze in my hands. Reveal the path, the truth that stands. Key of the gate, unlock and bind, open the door of spirit and mind."* Pause here for stillness. Gaze into the flames and allow Hekate to arrive.

Step 5: Declare the Crossroads Intention.

Stand at the center of the crossroads with your key in hand. Speak your current moment of transition aloud: *"I now stand at the crossroads, between what was and what may come. I call on Hekate to guide me through this choice, to set my boundaries, shield my will, and awaken the magick that walks beside me."* You may also write down your transition and place it beneath the key.

Step 6: Channel the Spell of Movement.

Hold your athame or hands over the key and say, *"With this spell, I claim the path. What must close, shall close. What must open, shall open. I walk forward with fierce grace, protected, guided, and reborn in sacred space."* Visualize the key glowing and the flames rising as your resistance softens into empowered direction.

Step 7: Close the Veil.

Thank Hekate, the dogs, serpent, and your own higher self. Blow out the candles. Take the key and place it somewhere intentional — in a pouch, on an altar, or on your person. To close say, *"The crossroads fade, but the flame remains. The spell is cast. The way is clear. By magick, by transition, and by resistance, my boundaries are sovereign. My will is strong."* Wipe or sweep away the crossroads marking as an act of sealing and release.

Essence

Truth

Bravery

Alchemy

Wisdom

Secrets

Prophecy

Enchantress

Dragonfly Echo

I step willingly into the cauldron of becoming. I face the fire with courage, stir the truth of my secrets within me, and choose transformation as my sacred path. I am not separate from the spell. I am its living breath.

14. Goddess Cerridwen

Energetic Invitation: Cerridwen, keeper of wisdom, spells, and ancient secrets, stirs the great cauldron of transformation — the sacred vessel where spirit, shadow, and substance merge into magic. She is the silent flame beneath the brew and the patient weaver of soul-shaping alchemy. As the revered enchantress of Welsh mythology, she is both goddess and guide — tender of thresholds and guardian of the deep mysteries that shape our becoming.

When Cerridwen calls, you are being summoned into a quieter power. Her medicine is not loud; it simmers. She does not command; she conjures. She invites you to sit beside her and investigate the swirling vapors of your own life. Truth bubbles to the surface only when you are still enough to see it rise. Bravery is not in the loud gesture but in the courage to sit with what is real.

This is the path of alchemy. It is slow, sacred work. Through Cerridwen's presence, you are asked to stir what has been stagnant, to heat what has been cold, and to transmute pain into deeper purpose. Her magic is the art of inner distillation — separating what no longer serves from the soul's true elixir.

She is the voice of wisdom that lives within your bones, the hum of ancestral knowing, and the rhythm of cycles that cannot be rushed. Prophecy flows from her cauldron not as prediction, but as remembering. You already carry the knowing — she simply awakens it.

Cerridwen does not offer easy answers. She offers sacred process. The only requirement is that you listen and trust what arises.

Shadow Path

When reversed, Cerridwen's presence may reveal a fear of transformation or hesitation to face an uncomfortable truth. You might sense her cauldron bubbling yet are afraid to peer into what it reveals, signaling a fear of your own inner wisdom or doubt that you can transmute pain into power.

You may be stuck in cycles of avoidance, clinging to comfort rather than stepping into the alchemy of change. The enchantress energy of Cerridwen becomes distorted when you suppress your own magic. She calls for honesty, but you may fear the truth will unravel what you have built.

Instead of wisdom, you encounter confusion. Instead of prophecy, you deny vision. And yet, she waits. In shadow, Cerridwen reminds you that what you fear may hold the very key to your becoming.

Symbolic Vision: Cerridwen stirs the glowing cauldron of deep alchemy, her hands tracing ancient patterns through the steam, her gaze steady and penetrating. This is no ordinary brew — it is the sacred elixir of soul transformation, where the elements of wisdom, truth, and prophecy converge in spirals of luminous heat.

Her cauldron, rooted in Welsh and Celtic mythology, is not merely a tool for spells — it is a living crucible, a sacred vessel through which divine alchemy unfolds. As the keeper of the sacred brew and guardian of secrets, she embodies the archetype of the enchantress, the wise woman who shapes reality through stillness, vision, and intentional stirring.

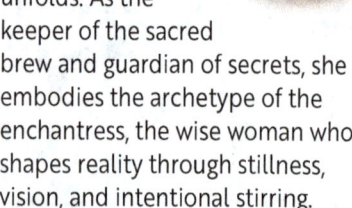

Above her the waning moon hangs like an ancient eye between gnarled branches, casting silver beams across the forest floor. This lunar glow illuminates cycles of surrender, retreat, and rebirth — echoing Cerridwen's rhythm as a goddess of both endings and sacred awakenings. The moon does not shine to rush your becoming. It watches patiently, reminding you that transformation brews best in silence and shadow.

At Cerridwen's side stands the revered white sow, a creature of deep

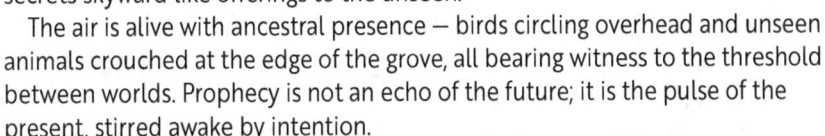

symbolic power in Celtic lore. The sow represents the fertile womb of the otherworld, the hidden subconscious brimming with nourishment and creative potential. While Cerridwen shapeshifts through form and flight, the sow remains rooted, an anchor of constancy in the cauldron's dance of change.

Cerridwen herself is the legendary shapeshifter who chased destiny through a tale of magical metamorphosis. From hag to hare, greyhound to otter, hawk to hen, her story in the myth of Taliesin is one of mystical pursuit, persistence, and sacred cunning. Her final transformation into a hen, swallowing the seed of prophecy, teaches that even the smallest forms carry the spark of divine consequence. Destiny often arrives feathered and quiet.

Around her sacred work grow potent herbs: vervain, rowan, mugwort, elder, sage, and lavender. These are not just plants — they are enchanted allies, each one humming with ancient resonance. Their scent curls with the sacred smoke that rises from the cauldron, carrying secrets skyward like offerings to the unseen.

The air is alive with ancestral presence — birds circling overhead and unseen animals crouched at the edge of the grove, all bearing witness to the threshold between worlds. Prophecy is not an echo of the future; it is the pulse of the present, stirred awake by intention.

Cerridwen does not demand. She waits. She watches. She brews. Her card is an invitation to enter the mystery, to trust the process, and to stir your own sacred truth from slumber.

Sacred Reflection

What is my guiding word, phrase, or image? Choose a symbolic essence. How can you honor this message daily through practice, art, or intention? Let it become your anchor — a sacred reminder that your transformation is becoming your truth.

Ritual

The Enchantress's Elixir

Supplies

- A small cauldron, fire-safe bowl, or stovetop pot
- A wooden spoon or ritual wand for stirring
- Representations of Cerridwen's animal forms (hen, sow; optional: hare, hawk, otter)
- Herbal blend: vervain, rowan, elder, mugwort, sage, lavender (Note: This is a symbolic potion. Do not ingest unless properly researched or guided by an herbalist.)
- A journal and pen
- Optional: incense, cloak, or sacred music

Step 1: Call the Enchantress.

Stand before your cauldron or pot. Take several deep breaths, filling your belly and softening your gaze. Root your feet into the earth. Let the room become still. Speak with intention, *"Cerridwen, great enchantress of the deep, stirrer of secrets, weaver of prophecy, and keeper of the ancient brew, I call upon you now. By the power of bravery, by the wisdom in shadow, guide me through the spiral of becoming."*

Visualize Cerridwen emerging from the mist, moonlight shimmering in her eyes. Feel her presence surround you — gentle, wise, and quietly powerful.

Step 2: Add the Herbs of Power.

Pour water into your cauldron. With each herb you add, speak aloud its sacred role in the transformation.

- Vervain: *"Open the inner eye to truth."*
- Rowan: *"Protect the path I cannot yet see."*
- Elder: *"Carry me through the fire of change."*
- Mugwort: *"Show me the secret written in my dreams."*
- Sage: *"Help me remember what I already know."*
- Lavender: *"Soothe and balance my soul."*

  Let the scent rise. Imagine your energy entwining with the potion.

Step 3: Stir the Cauldron of Secrets.

With your wooden spoon or ritual wand, stir the contents clockwise. Chant softly or aloud: *"Bravery in shadow, wisdom in flame, I stir the secrets that bear my name. By Cerridwen's brew, by moon and bone, I find the voice I call my own."* Let emotion surface. This is sacred alchemy.

Step 4: Witness the Prophecy.

Gaze into the steam as it curls upward. Allow images, thoughts, or feelings to emerge. Whisper, *"What does the enchantress show me now?"* Trust what comes. Record it in your journal. These are the whispers of your inner prophecy.

Step 5: Face the Flame of Bravery.

Place both hands on your heart, and say, *"I am not afraid to change. I am not afraid to know. What I stir, I become. What I release, sets me free."* Feel your courage rise.

Step 6: Close the Circle of Alchemy.

Say aloud, *"Cerridwen, enchantress, I thank you. Your wisdom echoes in my blood. The potion is complete. The spell is cast."* Let the brew cool. Return it to the earth in gratitude, completing the cycle.

Step 7: Anchor the Wisdom.

Place your hands over your heart or journal. Reflect on what you received. Choose one image or phrase, and create a sigil or write an affirmation. Say, *"I honor what I have seen. The enchantress walks with me."* Place this on your altar or within your sacred journal. Light a candle or anoint yourself with a drop of lavender or mugwort oil. Let the enchantment settle. You are the cauldron. You are the enchantress. Let your transformation begin.

Essence

Raven Magic
Protector
Augury
Shapeshifter
Battles
Sanctify

Dragonfly Echo

I rise in the dark and speak in storm light. I trust my voice, even when the wind howls against it. My destiny is not handed to me — I shape it with each breath. I walk with the goddess of prophecy and power. I do not fear endings; I become through them. I honor the fight, and sanctify the fire within me.

15. Goddess Morrigan

Energetic Invitation: When the Morrigan enters your field, she does not arrive with softness — she arrives with shadow magic. Her power does not destroy for destruction's sake — it reveals what must be stripped away for your spirit to rise. She calls forth the part of you that is ready to stand at the edge of transformation and not flinch.

Known as the Phantom Queen, the Morrigan is a powerful figure in Irish mythology. She is associated with fate, prophecy, and the sacred rites of war. Often appearing as a shapeshifter — a crow, raven, or sovereign warrior — she watches from the veil between worlds. She is both omen and oracle, protector and challenger.

This is your moment to sanctify your path, to make it holy through choice, courage, and unwavering self-truth. The Morrigan does not bring prophecy to soothe, but to awaken. What you see now is not just potential — it is your destiny calling. It will not wait forever.

She teaches that not all battles are fought with swords. Some are waged in the heart, in the mind, and in the reclaiming of your voice. If you have been avoiding the conflict within, she now stands before you — not to force you, but to mirror your power back to you.

To walk with the Morrigan is to remember your wild wisdom. You were not made to shrink. You were shaped to rise. With her as witness, you can shed your illusions and meet your fate with fierce grace.

You are the storm and the stillness. You are the warrior, and you are the fate.

Raven Magic • Protector • Battles • Augury
Shapeshifter • Battles • Sanctify

Goddess Morrígan

15

Shadow Path

When reversed, the Morrígan signals avoidance of truth, conflict, or destiny. You may be resisting an inevitable transformation, suppressing your voice when it is most needed, or clinging to roles that no longer serve.

You are being asked to confront your fear of endings and release the illusion of control. The prophecy has already arrived, but you haven't answered. This hesitation can distort your shadow magic, creating stagnation rather than sacred power.

You may be denying your shapeshifter nature, resisting the need to evolve. You were not born to retreat from battles of spirit. To sanctify your destiny, you must face the mirror, heed the signs, and claim the vision that has been waiting for your courage. The storm isn't punishment — it's your invitation.

Symbolic Vision: One crow and one raven rest in her grasp, with their talons curled around fate and wings veiled in ancient omens. Raised in each hand, they are not simply creatures but agents of reckoning and intuition. The crow, with piercing vision, sees through illusion and watches the decay of all that is complete. The raven, keeper of silence and shadow, flies the path of the unknown. Together, they confirm the Morrigan as both sentinel and storm — a guide through chaos and the still eye at its center.

Draped in night mist and bramble, the Morrigan moves between veils. She is the Phantom Queen, goddess of sovereignty, fate, and the sacred threshold between life and death. In Irish and Celtic lore, she rises as warrior queen, dark-winged guardian, and shapeshifter who wears prophecy like a cloak. Her presence is not chaos — it is the sacred pattern within it.

Above her a radiant pentagram pulses, etched in light and vibrating with ancestral memory. While she is more commonly known for her connection to ravens, crows, and the number three, the five-pointed star is a hidden key in her magic. This symbol of elemental harmony and spiritual command speaks to her deeper nature as not only destroyer but also balancer of forces.

Earth, air, fire, water, and spirit converge through her will, sanctified in power. The pentagram hums with ancient rhythm, reminding you that even war has its symmetry.

The Morrigan doesn't ask for fear — she asks for readiness. She appears when endings are inevitable, when illusions fall, and when truth must rise. She invokes shadow magic not as a curse, but as a crucible. She urges you to face your battles and walk the hard road of personal sovereignty. In her reflection, you are not broken — you are being reforged.

This goddess doesn't merely predict destiny— she invites you to claim it. Prophecy lives not in escape but in preparation. You are already receiving visions, signs, and symbols. The question is, Will you act on them? To stand in her presence is to be seen without pretense. To follow her call is to willingly enter transformation and choose bravery over comfort.

She does not comfort, she clarifies. She does not shield, she sharpens. She offers the sanctified storm. This is your threshold.

You are not meant to be small. You are meant to remember — to sanctify your voice, to embody truth, and to wield the alchemy of the shapeshifter within.

This is the Morrigan's mirror. Look in. The crow sees. The raven waits. The star burns. Your moment has come.

Sacred Reflection

What must I sanctify and protect at all costs? Explore what is sacred to you. What does the Morrigan teach you about guarding what matters most? What part of your life needs fierce protection and spiritual consecration now?

Ritual
Invoking Morrigan's Council

Supplies

- One black candle (truth and shadow)
- One white candle (sanctity and spiritual sight)
- A feather (preferably black),
- A dark crystal (obsidian, smoky quartz, or black tourmaline)
- Red string or thread
- A bowl of stormwater (rainwater or saltwater charged with intention)
- A small drawing or token of a pentagram (on paper, stone, or etched in salt)

Step 1: Cast the Circle of Sight.

Cast a sacred circle. Place the pentagram at the center of your ritual space as a symbol of elemental alignment and spiritual sovereignty. Visualize Morrigan's wings unfolding behind you. Hold your dark crystal and say, *"Morrigan, Phantom Queen of shadow and sovereignty, sanctify this circle in fate and flame. Guard me at this threshold where endings shape beginnings."*

Step 2: Light the Twin Flames.

Light the black candle to your left and the white candle to your right, forming a symbolic gateway. Each flame mirrors Morrigan's dual nature: war and wisdom, death and destiny. Whisper, *"With crow and raven, I rise between. By fire and void, I walk unseen."*

Step 3: Feel with the Feather of Prophecy.

Hold the feather above the flames without burning it. Feel it draw down insight from the unseen. Speak aloud the truth you are seeking or the shadow you are confronting. Invoke the Morrigan's gift of prophecy. Let the feather become a tool of augury and revelation.

Step 4: Channel with the Crystal of the Raw Self.

Place the crystal over your heart, and close your eyes. Ask, *"What is being called forth in me? What battles must I face to become?"* The Morrigan's truth is not comfortable — it is clarifying. Breathe deeply. Allow visions, memories, or truths to rise. Journal any messages that come through. Let her shadow magic expose what you must claim or release.

Step 5: Bind with Red Thread.

Wrap the red string around your wrist or fingers. It is a vow to destiny, an oath of sacred will. As you tie it say, *"I bind myself to the fire within — to my fate, to the storm, and to the truth that cannot be undone."* This is your soul's sanctified promise to follow the path, no matter how fierce.

Step 6: Anoint with Stormwater.

Dip your fingers into the stormwater. Touch your third eye, throat, and heart, activating vision, voice, and courage. Say, *"By storm and silence, I am sanctified. By wind and will, I rise unafraid."* Feel the water bless and awaken your soul's sovereignty.

Step 7: Release and Rise.

Hold the pentagram. Visualize it pulsing beneath your feet, connecting you to earth, spirit, and Morrigan's protection. Extinguish the flames and say, *"The crow has circled. The raven has flown. The truth is mine. And I rise, sanctified and sovereign."*

Keep the red thread until your intention manifests. Place the crystal on your altar or beneath your pillow. Let the pentagram remain until the next full moon, charged with the echo of your invocation.

Essence

Rebellion

Liberation

Unapologetic

Shadow Magic

Untamed

Bold

Dragonfly Echo

I unapologetically embrace my wild truth. I honor my sacred rage, my sexuality, and the fire that lives in my voice. I was never meant to be small. I am the untamed flame of liberation, the sacred witch of my own story. Now is not the time to hold back.

16. Goddess Lilith

Energetic Invitation: Lilith rises when the fire in your soul refuses to stay quiet — when rebellion becomes an act of truth. She is not here to be tamed or to comfort conformity.

Often described in ancient Jewish and Mesopotamian traditions as a dangerous spirit or demoness, she has evolved into a powerful symbol of unapologetic feminine force and sacred defiance. As the so-called first wife of Adam, Lilith chose exile over submission, refusing to be placed beneath him.

She is not a villain. She is a mirror for every woman who ever refused to shrink.

Lilith is shadow magic embodied — not because she is dark, but because she reveals the parts of us we were taught to fear. She sanctifies sexuality as divine force, not shame. She is the shapeshifter who dances on the edges of liberation, demanding we remember that wildness is holy. Her presence marks a return to your primal truth, unfiltered voice, and sovereignty.

When Lilith appears, you are being summoned into your own liberation. This is not a subtle path — it is a roaring one. Break the spell of silence. Tear down what cages you. Burn the contracts written in guilt and duty. This is the work of rebellion and rebirth.

You are not here to be palatable. You are here to be free. Stand in your unapologetic self. Let your sexuality be sacred. Let your shadow lead. You are the descendant of a goddess who shapeshifted through exile and made power out of fire.

Goddess Lilith

16

Shadow Path

When reversed, Lilith reveals the subtle ways you may be sacrificing your voice to feel loved or accepted. Are you shrinking in relationships, softening your truths to avoid judgment, or censoring your sensuality to meet someone else's comfort? This is not rebellion — it is restraint.

Shame may be whispering old scripts in your ear, but those stories are not yours. You are not too much; you are power unfiltered. This shadow calls you to confront your internalized conditioning and release what no longer belongs.

Lilith demands authenticity, not apology. Reclaim your voice, your wild, and your edges. Even in darkness, you are divine. Refusing to shapeshift to please others is the first act of liberation. There is power in being unapologetic.

Symbolic Vision: Lilith stands in a storm of her own summoning—hands outstretched, palms blazing with power, casting energy like wildfire through the unseen. Her touch does not ask for permission; it commands the very fabric of reality.

As the flames at her feet rise in rhythm with her breath, she radiates a pulse that ignites shadow magic, raw and immediate, felt in the bones, the blood, and the buried truth. Her black wings arch wide behind her, woven from midnight and myth, signaling her deep connection to dark and supernatural forces. They are not symbols of burden, but of flight — of freedom earned and truths reclaimed in the wild unknown.

Her long, untamed hair lashes around her shoulders like silk made from smoke, and the crescent moon gleams behind her — ever watching and shifting, a crown for the one who walks the threshold between seen and unseen.

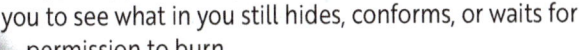

Her robes, the color of blood and embers, move like flame, whispering of trials endured and worlds undone. Adorned at her throat is a golden pentacle, not as ornament but as ward and weapon — a sigil of power, sovereignty, and sacred identity. Her eyes do not seek your approval; they challenge you to see what in you still hides, conforms, or waits for permission to burn.

Lilith is not a myth. She is a mirror, a memory, and a movement. She has been named demon, goddess, seductress, and sin. But those are merely labels given by the fearful. In truth, she is the wild origin of rebellion — the one who walked away from Eden with her head held high, choosing truth over silence. Her story is a spell of liberation, of becoming without apology, of standing in the heat of one's own fire and not flinching.

She is the voice of sacred rage — not destruction, but divine clarity. The rage that rises when you have been silenced too long — the heat that births the real you. She is the pulse of sovereignty that lives beneath your skin, calling you home.

She is not here to be softened or to wait. She is here to rise, and so are you. You are the smoke and the howl, the spell and the flame. You are the path and the reckoning. Shadow magic lives in your movement. You are the sacred act of rebellion becoming flesh, the living force of liberation, loud and lasting.

Sovereignty speaks through your voice, and your presence is the roar behind the silence, the storm behind the stillness. Say aloud, *"I belong to myself. I am the flame, and I will never be small again. I do not apologize."*

Sacred Reflection

What would it mean to live unapologetically? Describe the version of you who never dims, edits, or contorts to be accepted. What space do you claim? Let Lilith's flame light the truth of your unapologetic becoming.

Ritual

Unapologetic Becoming

Supplies
- A red or black candle (or both)
- A fire-safe bowl or cauldron
- A symbol of rebellion (ring, bone, chain, or talisman)
- Red lipstick, ash, or black kohl to draw on your body
- A private space to move, roar, and rise

Step 1: Light the Flame of Rebellion.

Light your candle, and stare into its blaze. Say, *"Lilith, I do not come to ask. I come to remember. Ignite the fire of my unapologetic becoming. Let rebellion rise in my bones."*

Let the flame awaken your wild core. Rebellion is not destruction — it is truth on fire.

Step 2: Cast the Circle of Bold Liberation.

With your arms or body, trace a circle around you. Visualize it glowing with red light. Say, *"This is not a wall. This is my liberation — a boundary of becoming where I answer only to my soul. I stand in my sovereignty untamed, whole, and real."* Let yourself expand fully, unfiltered and bold.

Step 3: Mark Yourself with Shadow Magic.

Use lipstick, ash, or kohl to draw a symbol or word on your throat, chest, or brow. Say, *"This is my shadow magic. Not hidden to shame, but honored to awaken. I do not deny what is mine. I bless it."* Mark your power. Make it visible. Let it sanctify the wild within.

Step 4: Burn the Mask of Obedience.

Write down a falsehood, a role, or a mask you have worn. Say, *"This mask never fit. I choose truth over silence and rage over suppression. This is my sacred rage. It is not wrong. It is holy."* Burn it. Let the smoke carry your rebellion into the ethers.

Step 5: Move Like a Bold Spell.

Dance. Stomp. Shake. Stretch. Roar. Let your body move like lightning. Say, *"I am the spell. I am the pulse. I move in rhythm with rebellion and grace. No one owns my body. I am liberation in motion."* Let your body reclaim its wild rhythm.

Step 6: Speak the Unapologetic Verse.

Let your voice ring out. Loud or whispered, make it real. Say, *"I will not apologize for my fire. I will not shrink to please. I will not fade to survive. I am sovereign. I am shadow and flame. I am the truth they tried to bury."*

Step 7: Seal the Fire, and Rise Untamed.

Blow out the candle with fierce presence — not to extinguish, but to internalize. Say,
"This flame is mine now.
It breathes in my rage, my joy, and my clarity.
I walk with Lilith. I rise with my power."

Step out of the circle and say, *"I carry the torch of Lilith's flame. I do not ask to exist. I arrive bold, wild, and free."*

Essence

Healing

Divine Magic

Sovereignty

Resurrection

Spellcaster

Dragonfly Echo

I carry the glyphs and tools of divine restoration. I call upon ancient magic to mend what has been broken and rise in the fullness of my sacred power. I am both the spell and the one who casts it. I am the hands that heal. I am the glyph written in gold. I am the living magic reborn.

17. Goddess Isis

Energetic Invitation: Isis, the radiant queen of sacred restoration, calls you home to the temple of your divine essence. She is not merely a figure of comfort — she is the spellcaster of transformation, the sovereign light within grief, and the resurrection after loss. Her magic is ancient and precise, a force that heals what others deemed irreparable.

A revered goddess in Egyptian mythology, Isis is honored as the divine magician, a healer, and the unwavering mother who gathered the dismembered body of Osiris and brought forth Horus through unwavering love and resurrection. She is the mother of sacred rebirth, the one who dares to believe that even broken things hold holy purpose. With every chant, with every sacred gesture, she reclaims what others abandon.

When Isis appears, she invites you to return to the parts of yourself you once lost, scattered through heartbreak, shame, or betrayal. She reminds you that healing is not linear; it is a sacred reclamation. Your voice, your presence, and your purpose are not gone; they are only dormant, waiting for your call.

You are being summoned into sovereignty, not as something to earn but as something to remember. You do not need to become worthy — you already are. Let Isis awaken the divine magic already in your hands. Let her pour her holy light into your wounds — not to erase them, but to empower you to weave your story with truth.

With Isis, nothing is ever truly lost. Everything is part of the spell. You are the restoration and resurrection.

Goddess Isis
17
Healing • Divine Majic • Sovereignty • Resurrection • Spellcaster

Shadow Path

When reversed, Isis reveals the places where you may be bypassing your pain, minimizing your sacred gifts, or placing your power in others' hands.

You may be waiting for permission to act, when in truth you are already chosen. You may feel disconnected from the sacred feminine within or from the wisdom that wants to flow through you.

Isis reminds you that healing is not passive; it is participatory. Restoration is not given; it is summoned. Even when you don't feel ready, you can begin.

Whisper your name to the temple walls. Let the goddess within awaken.

Symbolic Vision: With wings outstretched in perfect balance, Isis rises as a living glyph of sacred restoration. Her body becomes a spell — a portal between life, death, and rebirth — crowned with the solar disk and the horns of Hathor.

She is queen not just of Egypt, but of the unseen realms, standing at the threshold where ancient memory meets eternal power. Behind her, golden waves pulse like the Nile at sunrise, reminding us that she is the current of life itself. She weaves the elements through her feathers — green, blue, red, and black — colors of creation, shadow, and transcendence.

In Egyptian mythology, the wings of the goddess Isis primarily represent protection and resurrection. Her outspread wings were believed to shield the living and breathe life into the dead. On tomb walls and temple altars, her wings enfolded kings, souls, and sacred truths — offering safe passage between worlds. Her open wings form the symbol of divine guardianship, reminding all who call her name that the great mother does not abandon her children. She guards, heals, and resurrects.

Isis was a major goddess in ancient Egyptian religion, known for her powerful magic, healing abilities, and devotion to her family — especially Osiris and Horus. Her worship extended far beyond Egypt, echoing through the Roman Empire and across cultures as a beacon of sacred power and divine womanhood.

She is a queen whose name crossed oceans and centuries, carried by those seeking truth, comfort, and transformation. She is a powerful spellcaster — mistress of incantation and sacred rites. Through her voice, the dead were stirred. Through her hands, the broken were mended.

She not only possessed magic — she was magic, embodying divine magic in a way that shattered the boundaries between deity and mortal. Her very presence invoked healing and resurrection, not as myth, but as spiritual law.

The symmetry of her pose speaks to her sovereignty and her ability to command the forces of the universe while remaining rooted in grace and compassion. Her gaze does not waver. It looks beyond illusion, straight into the soul of the seeker.

You are being called to reclaim your sacred authority — to become both priestess and queen in your own life. Isis reminds you that healing is not passive; it is an act of power. Resurrection is not far away; it is a choice. And magic is not reserved for the initiated; it lives within your breath and bones.

Sacred Reflection

Where in my life have I experienced a resurrection — rising from loss, betrayal, or disconnection? Recall a time when life broke you open and forced you to rebuild. What strength, wisdom, or clarity did you reclaim through that transformation?

Ritual

Sacred Restoration

Supplies

- Myrrh and/or frankincense incense or resin
- Juniper, jasmine, or amber oil
- Rose petals
- Parchment paper and gold ink
- Blue candle
- Sacred herb (mugwort, sage, or lavender)
- Small bowl of water
- Your personal sigil or symbol of Isis.

Step 1: Begin Sacred Preparation.

Cleanse your ritual space with the rising smoke of myrrh and frankincense, sacred resins used in ancient Egyptian temples. Light a blue candle to welcome the divine presence of Isis, goddess of resurrection and celestial wisdom. Anoint your third eye and heart center with amber oil or lotus, whispering, *"I enter the temple of Isis, where divine magic flows and healing begins."* With this invocation, you align your soul with sacred intent and reclaim your inner sovereignty.

Step 2: Anoint the Body.

Blend sacred oils such as myrrh, juniper, or amber oil, long used for rites of resurrection. Gently anoint your hands, feet, heart, and crown while saying, *"With sacred oils, I awaken the vessel of healing. I summon resurrection through divine magic. I call forth my sovereignty with each sacred touch."* Feel your body become a living altar, ready to receive transformation.

Step 3: Write the Spell of Healing.

On parchment or consecrated paper, write in gold ink, *"By the power of Isis, I rise anew. In the name of the spellcaster, I summon healing. By divine magic, I am restored. Sovereignty is mine. Resurrection is now."* Sign and date it. Fold this sacred spell into thirds, and place it beneath a bowl of water charged by moonlight.

Step 4: Invoke Isis.

Stand tall, and raise your arms in the shape of Isis's winged glyph. Chant three times, *"Isis of the throne, divine enchantress, you who resurrected Osiris, bring your sacred breath to this spell. Let healing rise from the ashes and sovereignty awaken within me."* With each repetition, feel the pulse of divine magic filling your body.

Step 5: Offer the Sacred Herbs.

Add dried rose petals, lavender, or sacred herbs to your water bowl as an offering to Isis. Whisper, *"As these petals steep, so too shall resurrection stir what was lost. May divine magic renew me."* Leave the bowl beneath the moon overnight to empower your healing with lunar grace.

Step 6: Seal the Resurrection.

Take a few drops from the herb-infused water and anoint your forehead and heart. Add a final drop of rose oil, kyphi, or cinnamon — essences tied to passion and sacred devotion. Seal your parchment with a kiss, a sigil, or your personal glyph. Safely burn or bury it, completing your rite of resurrection.

Step 7: Affirm Sovereignty.

To close the ritual, say aloud, *"I am healed by holy hands. I am sovereign by sacred design. I am the spellcaster, risen and radiant. With Isis, I walk the golden path of resurrection."*

Blow out the candle. Sit in stillness. Let the divine magic settle into your bones and bless your path forward.

Essence

Love

Sacred Beauty

Magnetism

Pleasure

Sensuality

Charisma

Dragonfly Echo

I radiate sacred beauty from within. I honor my pleasure, magnetism, and softness as divine forces of power. I am a vessel of love and the embodiment of sensual sovereignty. I do not chase love — I attract it by being fully, fiercely myself.

18. Goddess Aphrodite

Energetic Invitation: When Aphrodite appears, the goddess of love calls you to return to the temple of your own pleasure, beauty, and sacred worth. She arrives not as a fantasy, but as a living force — an embodiment of love that begins with deep reverence for self. This is a call to soften without apology, to dress your emotions in roses and silk, and to treat your body as a temple of sacred beauty.

She invites you to drop the armor of shame and adorn your truth with grace. You are not too much. You are the magnetism of morning dew and twilight glow. To move in alignment with Aphrodite is to understand that your sensuality is a source of wisdom, not a sin. Sensuality, in her realm, is the language of the soul made flesh. It is where healing begins — not through denial, but devotion.

Aphrodite teaches that pleasure is a birthright, not a luxury. To sip beauty, to rest in softness, to honor your deepest yes — these are acts of rebellion and restoration. She doesn't ask you to be perfect. She asks you to be radiant, to become magnetic through joy, and to live charisma as an extension of authenticity.

Whether you are healing heartbreak, awakening desire, or reclaiming your power, Aphrodite holds the mirror gently and whispers, *"Let beauty bless your becoming."* Let every breath be a prayer of love. Let every touch be holy.

You are not meant to chase but to remember you are the temple others seek to enter.

Shadow Path

When reversed, Aphrodite reflects the tender places where your radiance has been dimmed or distorted.

You may be struggling to see your worth through a sacred lens, trading authenticity for approval, or chasing love rather than magnetizing it. This card calls attention to shame around sensuality, patterns of self-abandonment, or the belief that you must earn love by being less.

If you have been silencing your charisma, pleasure, or sacred beauty, it is time to clean the mirror. Aphrodite reversed is not rejection — it is a divine redirection, a sacred invitation to return to self-devotion and sovereignty. Your love, sensuality, and magnetism are not flaws to hide, but forces to reclaim. You are not meant to compete. You are meant to rise, adorned in your full divine essence.

Symbolic Vision: Aphrodite is not merely the goddess of surface allure; she is the keeper of beauty that births courage, the softness that holds power, and love that awakens soul remembrance. She stands luminous beneath a sky kissed by the peach, lavender, and rose hues of dawn. Her long golden-red hair flows like molten sunlight, caught in the breath of the breeze, as if the wind itself is drawn to her. Draped in silks of ivory and blush, cinched with a crimson sash, she is both grounded and ethereal — a goddess walking the edge between heaven and earth.

Aphrodite rises in a halo of sacred beauty, not simply adorned, but devotion incarnate. Her presence is magnetic, enfolding the space around her in sensual grace and radiant stillness. She carries the current of love not as fleeting emotion, but as a transformative force — a sacred frequency that inspires connection, reflection, and healing through presence and embodied truth.

The white dove nestled at her heart is more than a symbol of peace; it is the embodiment of pleasure as divine birthright. In Aphrodite's arms, softness becomes a strength that soothes, heals, and calls forth the soul. The dove whispers that intimacy, whether with self or another, is a holy act and a portal into deeper spiritual knowing.

Above her, another dove ascends into a lavender sky, with its wings wide with liberation. This is the soul, weightless in self-love, rising through the gentle pull of magnetism — not grasping, but drawing in what is aligned.

Her floral crown, woven with roses and laurels, hums with the vibrancy of sacred beauty. Roses, steeped in divine feminine magic, offer their fragrance like a spell — opening the heart, igniting sensual memory, and wrapping the senses in charisma. The laurel, once offered to victors, honors the power of the feminine to overcome, to inspire, and to reign without domination.

The sky behind her blooms with the pastels of Venus — rosy dawns and shimmering lavender — mirroring the hues of enchantment and grace. These colors, like the goddess herself, move like silk across the aura, cloaking her in the subtle brilliance of sensual power.

Aphrodite's eyes meet yours — steady, serene, and unflinching. Her gaze becomes a mirror, reflecting your own divine beauty, sacred worth, and pleasure as a path to wholeness. She speaks without sound, *"You are the spell."*

Her presence is a ritual of becoming, inviting you to peel back layers of shame, reclaim the joy of embodiment, and know without doubt that your desires are holy. She does not chase; she magnetizes. She teaches you to do the same.

Sacred Reflection

What does sacred beauty mean to me beyond appearance? How do you honor your inner radiance as divine? How can you turn daily rituals into expressions of reverence for the beauty that already lives within and around you?

Ritual

Shower or Bath of Sacred Beauty

Supplies

- Rose petals, hibiscus, or jasmine blossoms
- Sea salt or pink Himalayan salt
- A few drops of rose, vanilla, or jasmine oil
- A pink or white candle
- A mirror
- A rose quartz or other heart-centered crystal
- A silk scarf or soft towel
- Soft music or chimes

Step 1: Prepare the Waters of Beauty.

Whether taking a bath or shower, begin by creating a sacred atmosphere. Dim the lights. Light your candle. Play soft music or chimes. For a bath, fill the tub with warm water and sprinkle in salt and petals. Add a few drops of essential oil. For a shower, place herbs and salts in a sachet or bowl nearby, and add essential oil to the walls or floor where steam can carry it upward. Let your space become a temple of sensuality and sacred beauty.

Step 2: Invoke Aphrodite.

Before stepping in, place your hands on your heart and say aloud, *"Aphrodite, radiant muse of seafoam and fire, enter this sacred space of beauty and devotion. Show me the power of softness and the joy of knowing I am enough."* Feel her magnetism envelop you in warmth and divine presence.

Step 3: Cleanse and Anoint.

As you bathe or shower, slowly touch your body with loving awareness. Use your hands, a cloth, or even just the water to anoint your skin. Feel pleasure ripple through each caress. Whisper or repeat, *"I anoint myself with divine love. I am sacred. I am sensual. I am whole."* Let the water become both mirror and magic.

Step 4: Perform Mirror Affirmation

Afterward, wrap yourself in your scarf or towel. Stand before a mirror with the candle still glowing. Gaze deeply into your eyes and declare, *"I am beauty in motion. I am pleasure made holy. I am the spell."* Let your charisma rise and radiate outward.

Step 5: Express Gratitude and Release.

Offer Aphrodite your thanks aloud or silently. After a bath, allow the water to drain as a symbol of releasing shame, self-doubt, or comparison. After a shower, feel the final rinse wash away anything that clouds your sacred shine.

Step 6: Anchor the Magnetism.

Hold the rose quartz to your chest. Breathe deeply and say, *"My heart is a chalice of sacred love. I attract only what honors my beauty and truth."* Let sensuality awaken from within and ripple through your aura.

Step 7: Embody the Goddess.

Move through your space like a spell — graceful, magnetic, sovereign. Adorn yourself with silk, scent, or simply your bare skin. Aphrodite teaches that love begins within. You are radiant. You are enough. You are the pleasure. You are the spell.

Essence

Nurturing

Embodiment

Regeneration

Mother

Interconnection

Abundance

Dragonfly Echo

I am rooted, sacred, and whole. My body is a living altar of Earth's wisdom. I honor the cycles, the soil, and the breath of Gaia within me. Each step I take is an invocation of remembrance, a return to the sacred pulse of the living Earth. Mother Earth is calling me.

19. Goddess Gaia

Energetic Invitation: Gaia, the primordial soul of the Earth, rises now as a call to remember your deepest belonging. She is not merely the ground beneath your feet — she is the pulse in your bones, the rhythm of your breath, and the ancient knowing in your blood that whispers, *"You are not separate from nature. You are nature."*

Gaia is not only the mother of all; she is the mother within all. Her presence is both fierce and tender, reminding you that nurturing is not passive — it is powerful, regenerative, and holy.

This card arrives as an invitation to slow down and reconnect to the sacred truth of your embodiment. You are not a visitor here; you are woven into the fabric of the Earth's dreaming. Each inhale links you to the forests. Each heartbeat echoes the drum of ancient mountains.

You are not broken — you are becoming. Gaia teaches that true regeneration begins when we surrender to the cycles, trust the decay, and let old stories compost into new growth.

She invites you to return to your roots — not to retreat, but to rise with grounded grace. Bathe in moonlight. Listen to the water. Place your bare feet on soil, and remember that your body is holy terrain.

You are held. You are home. In her embrace, interconnection becomes the way forward, love becomes the medicine, and every cell in your being remembers the mother.

Gaia asks, *"Will you honor the sacred within by honoring the Earth around you? Will you live as though the planet is your altar?"*

Goddess Gaia
19

Shadow Path

When reversed, Gaia signals a sacred imbalance — a drifting away from the rhythms that once rooted you.

You may feel disconnected, anxious, overwhelmed, or cut off from your body's innate wisdom. This might manifest as chronic busyness, spiritual bypassing, or ignoring the vessel that carries your spirit.

You may find yourself living in overstimulated patterns, neglecting rest, nourishment, or time in nature. Perhaps you have forgotten the medicine of stillness, the grounding power of touch, or the pulse of the Earth beneath your feet.

Gaia reversed is a call to remember. Return to the soil of your being. Reclaim your body as a temple of interconnection. Let this be a reminder to come home to the mother within and around you!

Symbolic Vision: Before time wore a name, Gaia emerged from the swirling breath of chaos, not as a daughter of another force but as Earth herself. She is the great origin — the sacred ground from which all life rises.

From her womb came the sky, sea, mountains, and the first divine beings of creation. She is not simply a goddess of the Earth — she is the Earth.

Gaia is the cosmic mother of the Titans and the one who gave form to Uranus (sky) and bore the mighty beings who shaped the mythic ages. She birthed the Cyclopes, the hundred-handed Hecatoncheires, and countless deities of force and form.

Fertility, prophecy, and the pulse of nature move through her like blood in soil — ancient, knowing, and eternal. On this card, Gaia stands pregnant with the world — her full belly cradling the Earth like a sacred promise. This is not just a symbolic pregnancy; it is the embodiment of the truth that all things return to the mother, and all things are born from her. She is life in its totality: growth, decay, and rebirth.

Her posture is protective, powerful, and rooted like a mountain yet flowing like a river. Her long hair flows with elemental energy — fiery golden blonde strands blending with the deep blues of water and sky, reaching into the swirling cosmos behind her. Each strand carries the rhythm of wind, flame, tide, and stone, affirming Gaia's role as the interweaver of the five sacred elements: earth, air, fire, water, and spirit. Each symbol is etched around her like a celestial compass, anchoring her as the axis of all life.

Crowned with fresh daisies and green leaves, she wears the living world as her adornment. Her connection to the natural realm is not metaphor; it is reality. She is the breath in trees, the whisper beneath soil, and the pulse in the oceans. Gaia's body is landscape and temple alike.

This card radiates nurturing energy — an invitation to soften into the support of something larger than yourself. Gaia reminds you that to be human is to participate in a vast ecosystem of interconnection, where nothing is ever truly separate. Every inhale you take, every meal you consume, every step upon the Earth is a conversation with her spirit. She is embodiment in its most sacred form: to walk, create, hold life in your body, rest, and regenerate.

Gaia teaches that your very existence is an act of abundance — not because you must do more, but because you already are more, made of stars, soil, and soul. She does not rush. She does not compete. She roots, nourishes, and remembers. And in her stillness, all things grow.

Sacred Reflection

How do I nurture myself the way the Earth nurtures life?
Reflect on how you offer nourishment, rest, and loving attention to your body, emotions, and soul. How can your self-care more deeply mirror the Earth's steady, life-giving presence?

Ritual

Earth Mother's Embrace

Supplies
- Stones or leaves
- Fruit, seeds, or wild herbs
- A journal and pen (optional)
- A biodegradable object (such as a flower, strand of hair, or fruit)

Step 1: Return to Her.

Find a quiet place outdoors — ideally where you can walk barefoot, lie on the ground, or be near trees, stones, or flowing water. Before beginning, take a moment to thank the land aloud or in your heart. Whisper, *"I return to you, Mother."* Let your breath deepen. Feel the weight of your body. Drop into the now. Let the sky be your witness.

Step 2: Create the Circle of Connection.

Draw a small circle around yourself using stones, leaves, or your finger in the soil. This sacred boundary honors Gaia as both mother and mirror. As you stand or sit within it say aloud, *"I honor the web of life. I am part of the whole. I remember my interconnection."* Feel the pulse of the Earth beneath you. Know that you are never alone.

Step 3: Touch the Ground.

Place both hands on the ground with palms open. Offer your energy downward, and then draw energy up. This is the current of regeneration, a circuit of giving and receiving. Speak or think, *"May I be replenished by Gaia's grace. I release what no longer serves."* Let the soil take your burdens. Let the wind carry your sorrow.

Step 4: Nourish the Body.

Eat a small offering of fruit, seeds, or wild herbs as a sacred act of embodiment. Taste slowly. With each bite affirm, *"This is Gaia within me. I am nurtured. I am whole."* Let this remind you that your physical self is not separate from your spirit. It is part of the Earth's sacred abundance.

Step 5: Speak to the Mother.

Speak directly to Gaia, aloud or in writing. Ask for grounding, guidance, or renewal. You may wish to say, *"Great Mother, you who carry oceans in your belly and forests in your breath, root me in your wisdom. Let me rise through your love."* Listen in silence afterward. The breeze, a bird call, or the stillness itself may be her answer.

Step 6: Offer a Gift.

Leave behind something biodegradable as a token of gratitude: a flower, strand of hair, piece of fruit, or handwritten blessing. Whisper, *"May this return to you. May my actions honor the sacred balance."* This exchange deepens your interconnection and affirms the cycle of reciprocity.

Step 7: Walk the Spiral of Abundance.

To close, walk in a slow spiral outward from your circle, feeling each step as a return to the world with more presence. As you walk say softly, *"I carry Gaia's abundance. I am a vessel of nurturing. I walk the path of sacred embodiment."* Let the spiral open you to your day, reentering life as a priestess of Earth wisdom, grounded and alive.

20
Moon Phases

Cycles • Rhythm • Shadow • Illumination •
Spellwork • Eternal Dance

Essence
Cycles
Rhythm
Shadow
Illumination
Spellwork
Eternal Dance

Dragonfly Echo

I dance with the moon. My
energy waxes and wanes
with wisdom. In stillness, I
root. In fullness, I bloom.
I am the spell and the
tide. I am the light and
the shadow. These words
invoke my lunar essence.
I speak to them beneath
the stars, trace them in
moonlight on my skin, and
remember that I too am
made of celestial rhythm
and sacred mystery.

20. Moon Phases

Energetic Invitation: This card invites you to
align with the sacred cycles of the moon — the
oldest oracle known to witches, mystics, and seers.
Its phases speak the language of rhythm, ebbing
and flowing like the breath of the cosmos.

Just as the moon waxes and wanes, so too do
your energy, clarity, emotions, and magic. The lunar
current within you pulses with spellwork, drawing
you inward to reflect, and then outward to create.

You are not failing when you slow down. You are
moving in cycles, just as nature intended. Let yourself
retreat into the shadow of the new moon, where
seeds are planted in silence. Rise with the crescent,
expand under the full moon's radiant illumination,
and release with grace as the moon wanes.

The moon reminds you that time is not linear
— it is a spiral. You are not lost; you are becoming.
Trust your tides. Embrace your intuitive timing. Let
your magic be fluid and your healing be lunar.

When this card appears, it signals the need
to tune into your own eternal dance — a sacred
choreography with the stars. Each phase of the
moon becomes a mirror for your own becoming.
Are you birthing something? Shedding something?
Dreaming? Resting?

Let the moon phases awaken your inner oracle,
the one who dreams in shadow, howls under
moonlight, and weaves light into every crevice of
the soul. You are a vessel of cosmic rhythm — a
lunar being in motion. The moon is not distant; it
is dancing with you. Let it guide your magic.

Shadow Path

You may be resisting your natural rhythm — pushing forward when your spirit craves rest or shrinking back when it is your moment to shine. This resistance disrupts your energetic flow, leading to emotional overwhelm, spiritual fatigue, or a sense of disconnection from your intuition.

Perhaps you are forcing clarity when the moment calls for mystery or clinging to light when your soul needs to journey through the fertile dark. The moon teaches that every phase has purpose.

When reversed, this card signals to surrender to your inner lunar tide. Your magic is not gone; it is in a sacred pause. Trust the stillness. Honor the shadows as deeply as you honor the light. Like the moon, even in darkness you are in motion. Even when unseen you are on your way home.

Symbolic Vision: The Moon Phases card reveals the sacred choreography of time and transformation, offering a visual chant to the soul's spiral through cycles of light and shadow.

At the heart of the card glows the seven-pointed star (septagram) — a sacred sigil symbolizing unity, divine order, and soul evolution. Each of its seven points corresponds to a core frequency: body, mind, spirit, will, intuition, heart, and wisdom. This star anchors celestial rhythm into embodied purpose and aligns with the energetic matrix of the Earth. It is both compass and key, inviting you to move through your path with cyclical grace.

Surrounding the star is the complete lunar cycle, depicted as a radiant wheel.

Each phase holds its own portal of power:

- **New moon:** This time is a blank slate for intention-setting and seeding dreams. Use candle spells, manifestation rituals, and vision boards. What are you calling into being?

- **Waxing crescent:** Nurture your intentions with energy. Use charm bags, affirmations, or water charging to build momentum.
- **First quarter:** Act on your goals. Perform empowerment rituals, or invoke courage with fire-based magic.
- **Waxing gibbous:** Refine and prepare. This phase is ideal for divination and enchantment work. Clarify what needs adjusting before the full moon.
- **Full moon:** This is a peak time of power, celebration, and clarity. Perform ritual baths, crystal charging, or rituals of gratitude. This is a time of energetic culmination and spell amplification.
- **Waning gibbous:** Release what no longer serves. Use herbal smoke or flame to banish stagnation and honor your lessons.
- **Last quarter:** Reflect and forgive. Journaling, cord-cutting, and ancestral offerings are powerful now.
- **Waning crescent:** Rest, dream, and commune with the void. Sleep magic, oracle reading, and spirit connection are encouraged.

Encircling the moon wheel is a luminous orange band etched with the Theban alphabet — the witches' alphabet. This ancient magical script is a language of secrecy and sacred intention, reminding us that spellwork begins with the word. Whether spoken aloud or whispered in silence, our language weaves reality.

Surrounding this is a yellow ring marked with the Roman alphabet, representing conscious communication and the mundane made magical. These dual rings symbolize the bridge between the seen and unseen, the spell and the sentence, and the sigil and the syllable.

In each corner of the card, intricate Celtic knots in green, red, blue, and purple echo the four elements — earth, air, fire, and water — grounding the moon's shifting phases into elemental truth. These woven symbols reflect the eternal cycle of life, death, and rebirth.

This card calls you into the eternal dance of lunar rhythm and personal magic — an ever-turning spiral of cycles, illumination, shadow, spellwork, and magic energy.

Sacred Reflection

How do I experience emotional, spiritual, or energetic change throughout the moon's cycle? How can you better align with your body's natural rhythm rather than resisting it? Which lunar phase calls to you most right now, and why?

Ritual

Moon Rituals

Supplies
- Cleansing: sage, incense, sound, saltwater, moon water, earth, salt
- Crystals (smoky quartz or obsidian, carnelian or citrine, tiger's eye or red jasper, moonstone or selenite, amethyst, fluorite, lepidolite or larimar)
- Candles (black, green, red, yellow/gold, white/silver, blue, purple, silver/dark blue)
- Herbs: rosemary, lavender
- Paper or parchment

Ritual 1: New Moon Ritual

Cleanse your space with smoke or water. Ground through breath. Set a clear intention for the new cycle. Light a black candle with smoky quartz or obsidian nearby. Write your wish on parchment, visualizing it sinking into the fertile void. Bury or place it beneath your crystal. Close with gratitude and silence.

Ritual 2: Waxing Crescent Ritual

Purify your altar with incense or sound. Center your energy with steady breath. Focus on growth through small actions. Light a green candle with carnelian or citrine nearby. Write a short affirmation, and chant it as the flame glows. Place it on your altar to charge. Reflect on your inspired next step.

Ritual 3: First Quarter Ritual

Cleanse with saltwater or herbs. Stand grounded. Set an action-driven goal. Light a red candle with tiger's eye or red jasper nearby. Write one fear and its opposite strength. Burn the fear, and keep the strength. Meditate on courage, offer thanks, and then take a bold aligned action in the days ahead.

Ritual 4: Waxing Gibbous Ritual

Cleanse ritual tools. Reflect quietly on progress. Refine your intention or clarify direction. Light a yellow or gold candle with citrine or moonstone nearby. Write a vow of commitment, and speak it aloud. Charge your tools or journal beneath the flame. Breathe deeply, anchoring renewed focus and devotion to your unfolding path.

Ritual 5: Full Moon Ritual

Cleanse your aura with moon water or smoke. Stand barefoot or hold moonstone or selenite at your heart. Focus on what has ripened. Light a white or silver candle. Write gratitude or manifestations, read them aloud under the moon, and then burn them. Dance, sing, or sit in joy, honoring radiant wholeness.

Ritual 6: Waning Gibbous Ritual

Cleanse your space with rosemary or lavender. Reflect on insights revealed. Focus on graceful release. Light a blue candle with amethyst or fluorite nearby. Write what you are ready to let go of. Tear or burn it, scattering ashes on the earth. Seal the ritual with a calming breath and a simple prayer of gratitude.

Ritual 7: Last Quarter Ritual

Cleanse your altar with earth or salt. Reflect on the cycle's lessons. Set closure or forgiveness intentions. Light a purple candle with amethyst neaerby. Write a forgiveness letter to yourself or another. Read it, and then burn it. Pour water over the ashes, grounding them into the earth. Offer silent thanks for healing and release.

Ritual 8: Waning Crescent Ritual

Cleanse your body with a ritual bath or shower. Enter stillness and rest. Set intention for inner renewal. Light a silver or dark blue candle with lepidolite or larimar nearby. Write a dream for the next cycle, and sleep with it beneath your pillow. Record your dreams on waking. Thank the moon, and reset.

21. Cosmic Blueprint

Essence
Astrology
Destiny
Soul Map
Sacred Timing
Cosmic Weaver

Dragonfly Echo

I am made of stars, encoded with celestial wisdom. My soul weaves in rhythm with the cosmos. I trust the map of my becoming and walk in harmony with divine timing. Each transit is a call to align with truth. My chart is not fate; it is sacred language. I am the alchemist of my destiny, illuminated by light.

Energetic Invitation: You are not separate from the stars—you are composed of them. The stardust in your veins is a reminder that astrology is not merely a study—it is your birthright.

The wisdom of the cosmos lives within your cells, your dreams, and your breath. The Cosmic Blueprint card arrives as a luminous mirror, reflecting the encoded language of your soul's destiny.

At the moment of your birth, the universe crafted a divine design: your natal chart. This chart is your soul map, a sacred navigational key to understanding who you are, why you came, and what you are here to embody. These planetary placements are not fixed instructions, but invitations to unfold your unique path with grace and awareness.

You are the cosmic weaver, braiding past, present, and future into an evolving pattern of awakening. Astrology doesn't control you; it speaks to you. It offers you tools, timing, and truth. Sacred timing is written in the skies, and yet you always hold the thread. Retrogrades slow us for review, transits guide us toward new chapters, and returns bring cycles of completion and rebirth.

This card asks you to tune into those celestial rhythms. What house are you walking through now? What archetype is being activated within you? Whether you study charts or simply feel into lunar tides, your awareness is the ceremony.

You were born for this moment. You are not here by accident. You are the sky in motion — living art, divine mathematics, and infinite potential incarnate.

Cosmic Blueprint
21

Shadow Path

Reversed, this card may indicate a sense of disorientation, confusion, or a disconnection from your soul's purpose. You may find yourself questioning your path or doubting your inner knowing, seeking external validation through charts, horoscopes, or predictions.

While astrology offers guidance, it is not meant to replace your own intuition. You may feel overwhelmed by cosmic data instead of trusting the sacred timing unfolding within.

Are you allowing the stars to guide you or rule you? Perhaps you are resisting your soul map, thinking destiny is fixed rather than fluid. Let the stars be a reflection, not a restriction. The map is not outside you. It is etched in your breath, your choices, and your becoming. Trust your cosmic blueprint.

Symbolic Vision: A radiant zodiac wheel turns across the velvet sky, constellations glowing like ancient sigils of soul memory. Each sign pulses with archetypal light — names etched in celestial ink, glyphs humming with wisdom.

At the center, the sun and moon spiral in sacred union — light and shadow dancing in balance, threading your destiny. Around them, planets orbit like silent messengers, weaving the ever-evolving tapestry of your soul map. This is the Cosmic Blueprint — a living mandala of astrology and sacred timing.

You are not separate from this pattern; you are composed of it. Your natal chart is not just a tool; it is a mirror, a sacred contract, a remembrance. It reveals your light, shadow, strengths, and soul's evolution. By aligning with this soul map, you amplify your gifts, soften your challenges, and walk your path with clarity and compassion. You are written in stars and stardust. You are the blueprint.

Aries
Light: Initiates with bold fire, igniting action with fearless presence
Shadow: Can act without thought, burning bridges in haste or pride

Taurus
Light: Grounds in abundance, loyal to love and the sensual world
Shadow: May resist change, clinging to comfort or stagnation

Gemini
Light: Dances with ideas, quick-witted and curious, a messenger of air
Shadow: May scatter focus or use words to distract rather than connect

Cancer
Light: Moves with moonlight, nurturing deeply from an intuitive core
Shadow: Can retreat into emotional armor, fearing vulnerability

Leo
Light: Radiates sovereign warmth, leading with creativity and heart
Shadow: May seek approval or dim others in the quest to shine

Virgo
Light: Heals through clarity and sacred service, a steward of detail
Shadow: Can overanalyze or fall into perfectionism and self-critique

Libra
Light: Balances love, beauty, and fairness with grace and connection
Shadow: May avoid truth or lose self in the quest to keep peace

Scorpio
Light: Transforms through emotional depth and spiritual rebirth
Shadow: Can withhold truth, manipulate, or control

Sagittarius
Light: Explores with joy, igniting minds and paths with optimism
Shadow: May chase freedom without focus or run from emotional depth

Capricorn
Light: Builds with steady wisdom, carving sacred ambition into reality
Shadow: Can become rigid or sacrifice joy to meet impossible standards

Aquarius
Light: Channels innovation and truth from the future into now
Shadow: May detach from emotion or become lost in the abstract

Pisces
Light: Dreams in divine unity, softening separation with compassion
Shadow: Can dissolve boundaries, losing clarity in fantasy or martyrdom

Sacred Reflection

What does my astrology reveal about divine timing in my life? Reflect on current transits — Saturn returns, Venus retrogrades, and lunar nodes. Are you surrendering to divine pacing, resisting its flow, or learning its sacred wisdom?

Ritual

Awakening the Zodiac Within

Supplies
· Mugwort or frankincense
· 12 small stones, shells, or zodiac tokens
· A white candle
· A crystal or grounding tool
· A journal or parchment
· A symbol of your intention (e.g., flower, feather, crystal, or coin)

Step 1: Align Sacred Space.

Cleanse your space with smoke or sound using mugwort, frankincense, or chimes. Place a circle of 12 small stones, shells, or zodiac tokens in front of you, representing the signs of the zodiac. At the center, set a white candle to represent your inner star. As you light it say, *"I call upon the cosmic blueprint within me. May the stars above awaken the wisdom below."*

Step 2: Ground in the Present Sky.

Hold your favorite crystal or grounding tool. Take three deep breaths and connect to this moment. Visualize the wheel of the zodiac above your crown, spinning slowly in starlight. Speak aloud your birth sun sign, moon sign, and rising sign. Feel their presence anchor you into both earth and sky.

Step 3: Call in the 12 Archetypes.

One by one, name each zodiac sign aloud. As you speak them, envision their essence circling around you like constellations: Aries the flame, Taurus the root, Gemini the wind, Cancer the tide, Leo the sunbeam, Virgo the healer, Libra the breath of balance, Scorpio the deep water, Sagittarius the fire arrow, Capricorn the sacred climb, Aquarius the future spark, and Pisces the dreaming sea. Affirm, *"Each of these lives in me. I welcome their light and lessons."*

Step 4: Reflect on the Star Map.

On parchment or in your journal, draw a simple zodiac wheel or note your birth placements. Choose one planet and sign pairing that feels potent today (e.g., moon in Scorpio, Venus in Leo). Reflect, *"How is this energy guiding my current path? What strength or shadow is being illuminated?"* Write freely. Let insight flow.

Step 5: Activate the Cosmic Heart.

Place your hands over your heart. Repeat this mantra: *"I am a sacred weaver of light and shadow. I honor my soul map. I walk in rhythm with the stars."* Visualize threads of silver starlight moving from your chest out into the heavens, connecting you to the divine rhythm of astrology, destiny, and sacred timing.

Step 6: Offer to the Sky.

Choose a symbol of your intention (e.g., flower, feather, crystal, or coin) and place it outside under the stars or on your altar. Whisper, *"As above, so within. As I honor my cosmic blueprint, I align with the flow of creation."* This anchors your ritual into the web of time and space.

Step 7: Close and Integrate.

Blow out the candle. Sit in silence. Let the archetypes you have invoked settle into your being. Write a final reflection: *"Today I walk with the stars. I trust my divine design. I am becoming."* Close with gratitude, knowing you are a living sky.

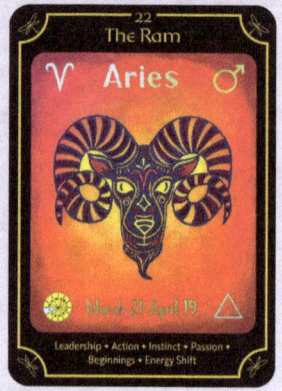

Element: Fire
Ruling Planet: Mars
House: First (identity, will, direction)
Essence: *Leadership ✦ Action ✦ Instinct ✦ Passion ✦ Beginnings ✦ Energy Shift*

Dragonfly Echo

I am the spark that starts the fire. I lead with boldness and act with sacred certainty. My courage is the doorway to transformation. I am fearless and courageous. I take inspired action and lead with confidence, knowing that the universe supports my bold steps.

22. Aries: The Ram

Energetic Invitation: Aries arrives as the initiator of the zodiac and is ruled by Mars, the planet of drive, intensity, and raw momentum.

As the first sign in the astrological wheel, Aries embodies ignition, fearless beginnings, and the wild pulse of life in motion. This is the fiery essence of the first house: identity, will, and direction. Aries energy surges forward, daring and undeterred. It doesn't wait for permission; it acts, builds, and forges paths where none existed before.

This card signals a powerful energy shift, stirring your spirit toward boldness and unapologetic movement. You are being called to embrace leadership, not as a position of control, but as a sacred act of self-trust.

Aries invites you to claim your space, to lead not from ego but from unfiltered instinct. The wisdom of Mars fuels your inner fire, offering the passion required to push through resistance and breathe life into dormant dreams.

Where in your life are you being urged to move first, to start now, to trust the flare of your inner vision? Action is the portal. This card dares you to begin, even when the full path isn't visible. Your soul already knows the next step.

Aries reminds us that courage isn't waiting until we're ready — it's the magic of beginning before certainty arrives.

Let this be your season of fierce beginnings, of igniting purpose, and of stepping boldly into the unknown. Trust that the flame you carry will light the way forward.

♈ Aries ♂

March 21 - April 19

Shadow Path

When Aries appears reversed, it may reveal burnout, impulsive reactions, or the urge to dominate rather than lead. Mars energy, when misdirected, loses its sacred edge — action becomes erratic or aggressive and no longer rooted in truth. You may be charging ahead without vision or retreating in fear, missing the instinct that once guided you.

The shadows of beginnings arise when we rush or resist the call to evolve. This imbalance signals a deep energy shift — a need to recalibrate before pushing further. Is your fire fueled by true passion, or is frustration running the show?

Pause. Reflect. Aries teaches that even in darkness you can realign. This is the moment to reclaim your power and begin again — consciously, compassionately, and with integrity.

Symbolic Vision: The ram surges forth from a blazing orange and red horizon, its spiral horns engraved with radiant patterns that shimmer with sacred geometry and celestial intelligence. Each curve holds a frequency, a cosmic echo of power encoded through time. This is more than animal instinct — it is ancestral knowing.

The gaze of the ram is unwavering, with its eyes burning with purpose, intention, and ancient clarity. This is the soul mid-leap, awakening to its own fire.

Above the ram the Aries glyph glows beside the sigil of Mars — both blazing in the heavens like celestial firebrands. The ruling planet Mars surges with desire, conviction, and divine will. It does not ponder; it propels. Its essence flows through the ram's every movement: in the strike of its hooves, the arc of its horns, and the momentum of its charge. Mars is the initiator and the divine activator of will. The element of fire, alive and fierce, crackles through the scene uncontained, yet not chaotic. It is the heat of creation — the first spark of transformation.

Below the ram the emblem of the first house pulses with luminous resonance, anchoring this mythic energy into the zodiacal wheel. The first house of identity, will, and direction governs how we enter the world and how we assert "I am." This is the domain of self-definition, of becoming visible, and of being.

The triangle of flame at the base radiates solar fire and elemental power, an emblem of inspiration, initiation, and instinctual presence.

The Aries archetype does not arrive gently. It ignites. Its essence is leadership, action, instinct, passion, beginnings, and energy shift. These are not merely characteristics — they are a blueprint. Leadership in Aries is not about control; it is the courage to act first, to light the path no one else dares to walk. Action is sacred here with movement as ritual and choice as destiny. Instinct becomes oracle, a trusted flame in the dark. Passion is the fuel, the wild force that makes the leap possible. Beginnings are holy ground, the moment before form when potential becomes kinetic. And the energy shift is the initiation — the threshold between who you were and who you are becoming.

Courage, leadership, action, independence, passion, impulsivity, and initiative are not mere words. They are vibrational truths, woven into the mythic ram's DNA. Aries doesn't ask. It dares. It moves with divine fire and sacred defiance.

Aries in its purest form is the spark of becoming, the battle cry of birth, and the first breath that declares "I am."

Sacred Reflection

How can I take one inspired step this week toward something that lights me up? Ground your vision into motion with bold intention. What small, courageous action can you take that honors your fire? Let desire lead. Begin where passion meets purpose.

Ritual

Ignite Your Inner Flame

Supplies

- *Red candle (for fire and initiation)*
- *Carnelian, red jasper, and fire agate crystals*
- *Fresh rosemary sprig or essential oil*
- *Fire-safe bowl or cauldron*
- *A bell or chime*
- *Journal or paper*

Step 1: Sacred Spark (Open the Portal)

Light your red candle, and sit with your carnelian in your left hand. Breathe deeply into your belly, feeling the flame of will rise through your core. Whisper, *"I call forth the flame of Aries within me. Let my will rise like the dawn — unyielding, radiant, and pure."* Let your inner fire stir awake, crackling with intention and impulse.

Step 2: Circle of Flame (Cast the Container)

Anoint your temples and wrists with rosemary. Place the red Jasper at the southern edge of your space, anchoring your fire. Trace a protective circle around your space with your hand or wand while saying, *"In the name of bold beginnings, I set this space apart. Let my passion be grounded and fierce."* You have entered the sacred forge of your becoming.

Step 3: Embers of Intention (Write the Spell)

Write down one clear, bold declaration — your Aries desire — in present tense. Let it roar from your gut. For example, *"I act on my soul's calling with fearless clarity."* Fold it three times, and place fire agate on top of it to charge it with protection and truth.

Step 4: The Flame Rises (Light the Fire)

Burn the folded paper in the fire-safe bowl. As smoke spirals upward whisper, *"With fire I forge, with fire I release. This flame carries my will beyond fear."* You have now activated the fire of transformation.

Step 5: Warrior's Breath (Practice Embodiment)

Stand tall in your warrior stance, holding carnelian near your solar plexus. Take three deep warrior breaths — inhale through the nose, exhale forcefully through the mouth. Feel your energy field ignite, pulsing with purpose and momentum.

Step 6: Ring of Victory (Seal the Spell)

Place all three crystals in a triangle around your candle. Ring your bell or tap your cauldron and say, *"The flame is lit. The way is clear. By Aries' light, I boldly steer."* Allow the candle to burn through, or extinguish it safely with gratitude.

Step 7: Reflection Flame (Write Sacred Reflection)

Write in your journal using this prompt: *What within me longs to begin, and what fire must I walk through to claim it?*
+ I let the flame show me the truth beneath hesitation. I trust my instincts. I act when the moment is ripe.
+ How do courage and grounded presence shape my sacred becoming?

Element: Earth

Ruling Planet: Venus

House: Second (finance, material possessions, self-worth, pleasure)

Essence: *Decadent ✦ Loyalty ✦ Family ✦ Grounded ✦ Stubborn ✦ Career ✦ Worth*

Dragonfly Echo

I am grounded and abundant. I trust in the steady process of spiritual growth and career and embrace the pleasures of life with gratitude. What I nurture flourishes. I honor my pace, knowing that slow roots grow the strongest blooms.

23. Taurus: The Bull

Energetic Invitation: Taurus enters your reading as a sacred reminder: You are not meant to rush — you are meant to root.

As the second sign of the zodiac, Taurus embodies the sacred Earth and is ruled by Venus, goddess of beauty, abundance, and worth. She arrives like the slow bloom of spring — anchored, sensual, and serene. The bull does not run. It plants, builds, and tends. Its presence is your call to slow down and tune in to the rhythms of your body, the weight of your breath, and the pleasure of the present moment.

Associated with the second house of astrology — governing self-worth, material stability, finances, and pleasure — Taurus asks, What are you cultivating? What are you consuming? Does it honor your value? It teaches that true beauty begins within and is reflected outward through devotion to what is real.

This is not indulgence for indulgence's sake. This is sacred preservation. When you prepare food with intention, nourish your body with rest, and surround yourself with softness, you are engaging in spiritual service. Stability, patience, and sensuality are not obstacles; they are oracles.

Career, family, and creative work are not rushed but built brick by brick with presence. Worth is not proven through hustle but embodied through devotion.

Taurus reminds you to come home to what you love, to bloom without force, to honor your body as holy ground, and to root deep in what is real.

Let this be your season of softness. Let beauty be enough. Let your worth speak without needing permission.

Taurus

 April 20 - May 20

Shadow Path

The shadow of Taurus appears when the desire for comfort becomes a cage. You may be resisting change, clinging to what is familiar, or tethering your self-worth to productivity.

When the bull digs in out of fear, stagnation replaces stability. This shadow can manifest as workaholism, possessiveness, financial hoarding, or emotional inertia. If you are overextending to prove your value or holding tightly to routines, relationships, or roles that no longer nourish you, pause and ask, What am I gripping that no longer grounds me?

Taurus teaches that people are not possessions and success is not sustained through burnout. True abundance includes rest, ease, and the courage to receive without guilt. What if the ground you fear losing is the compost for your next bloom?

Symbolic Vision: In a luminous field of emerald green, the sacred bull rises — a living sigil of patience, power, and sensual devotion. Its form is carved from the earth's memory, and its body is dense with grounding wisdom.

Etched across its broad face are golden patterns — ancient Venusian markings and sacred geometry of worth and beauty, drawn not in haste but through centuries of care.

Its crescent-shaped horns curve like lunar gateways, portals of instinct and preservation. Atop its brow rests a gleaming pyramid, a beacon of authority and ancient knowing. This is not power that roars; it resonates.

The bull holds the quiet command of Earth: magnetic, steady, and sovereign. Around it drift soft glowing orbs — Pleiadian stars, reminding us that the bull's love of beauty and indulgence can be deeply cosmic when approached with reverence. Hearts appear at the nose — not decoration, but a sacred code. They symbolize the rulership of Venus, the planet of love, beauty, and material harmony.

This is not a cold creature of survival; it is a protector of family, a steward of stability, and a builder of beauty. When Taurus works, it does so out of love. When Taurus rests, it regenerates the world.

This earth sign rules the second house of astrology, governing finance, career, self-worth, material possessions, and the pleasures that nourish both body and spirit. The bull reminds you that your value is not just in what you do but also how you receive.

Taurus does not chase; it draws. Through grounded presence and unshakable devotion, Taurus magnetizes abundance. The bull's essence is loyalty, family, and worth.

Its stubbornness is not resistance but loyalty to what truly matters. Taurus shows up daily, silently, and loyally to care for its family, build lasting legacies, and transform the material into the sacred.

Indulgence is not forbidden here. It is holy — a soft robe. a full pantry, and a moment of stillness in the sun. These are not luxuries; they are the rituals of a life well loved.

The bull invites you to see your body as the altar, your home as the temple, and your time as sacred ground. You are not here to prove worth. You are here to embody it. You are not meant to rush. You are here to root. The earth cradles your becoming.

Taurus teaches that presence is prosperity. You are the fertile field, the bloom, and the bounty. You are the keeper of sacred rhythm.

Sacred Reflection

What legacy am I building, and is it aligned with what I truly value? Taurus builds slow, lasting structures. Are your current habits, relationships, or career choices part of the sanctuary you wish to create? How might devotion, not dut, reshape your foundation?

Ritual

Embodiment of Worth

Supplies

- Crystals: *rose quartz, emerald, green aventurine*
- Earth element: *soil, salt, or stone*
- Fresh flowers: *roses, sunflowers, peonies, or your favorite*
- Luxurious fabrics: *silk, lace, velvet, linen, or anything sensually comforting*
- Physical money: *coins or bills*
- Scented oil: *amber, rose, or patchouli*
- Indulgent food: *fruit, honey, chocolate, or something rich and meaningful*
- A candle

Step 1: Create Your Venusian Sanctuary.

Craft a sacred altar space that reflects the sensual essence and Venusian magic of Taurus. Arrange your crystals alongside fresh flowers, and include an earth element. Lay out soft, luxurious fabrics, and place a few coins or bills as a symbol of abundance. Add your chosen oil and a small plate of indulgent food. Light a candle to signify the spark of devotion. As you gaze into the flame say, *"I enter the temple of my own worth. I surround myself with sacred beauty and call upon Venus to awaken the power of pleasure and peace within me."*

Step 2: Root into the Earth.

Step outside or stand barefoot on the floor. Touch the earth or hold a grounding stone. Close your eyes, and draw long, slow breaths into your belly. Feel the weight of your body sinking into support. Say, *"I root into the earth. I honor my pace. I grow slowly and strong."* Visualize golden roots extending from the soles of your feet or spine, reaching deep into Earth's core, anchoring you in steady, nourishing calm.

Step 3: Anoint and Awaken the Body.

Slowly and reverently anoint your skin with oil, beginning at the feet. As you touch each part of your body say, *"This body is sacred. This body is home. This body is a temple of pleasure."* Wrap yourself in your chosen fabric, allowing softness and comfort to become your second skin. Let your body feel adorned and adored.

Step 4: Make a Pleasure Offering.

Choose a small portion of your indulgent food, and taste it as if it were a sacred offering. Let each bite become a devotion. Move gently — sway, stretch, or let your body respond intuitively. Run your fabric or a soft object across your skin and say, *"I allow myself to feel. I allow myself to receive. Pleasure is my prayer and spell."*

Step 5: Activate Self-Worth.

Hold your coins or bills and declare, *"I am worthy of abundance, love, and laughter simply by being. I do not chase worth; I embody it."* Pause and reflect on what makes you proud, and then whisper, *"My worth is not earned. It is remembered."*

Step 6: Rest in Sacred Stillness.

Lie down or sit in stillness. Envision a golden light surrounding you, entering your aura with warmth and peace as you say, *"As I rest, I receive. As I soften, I expand. I am a sanctuary of love and grace."* Let your nervous system melt. Let receiving become the spell.

Step 7: Close in Gratitude.

Slowly blow out your candle. Place one hand over your heart and the other one on your forehead. Take a breath in and say softly to yourself, *"I honor myself. I am whole. I am enough."*

Element: Air

Ruling Planet: Mercury

House: Third
(communication,
intelligence, environment)

Essence: *Inquisitive ✦
Curious ✦ Adaptable ✦
Duality ✦ Charming ✦
Gossip ✦ Versatile*

Dragonfly Echo

I embrace duality as
wisdom. My words are
spells, and my curiosity is
a guide. I return to clarity
and truth. In dialogue
with self, Spirit, and life,
I awaken. I am not just a
voice; I am vibration, alive
and becoming.

24. Gemini: The Twins

Energetic Invitation: The Gemini card invites you
to attune to the sacred element of air — the breath
of communication, thought, and connection. As
the sign of the twins, Gemini is a cosmic mirror,
reflecting duality not as conflict, but as a sacred
dance of possibility. Ruled by Mercury, the planet
of language and transmission, Gemini is the
messenger between realms, the storyteller, and
the weaver of paradox into poetry.

When Gemini appears, you are called into
dialogue with life. This is a season to speak, listen,
question, and exchange. Gemini governs the third
house of communication, environment, perception,
and mental rhythms. It awakens intelligence,
curiosity, and the magic of noticing what others
miss. You are being guided to explore your
multidimensional self and to honor the inquisitive
and adaptable parts of you that thrive in flexibility.

If you have felt stagnant, indecisive, or tongue-
tied, Gemini breathes fresh perspective into
your field. Words are spells now. Conversations
are rituals. Ideas are portals. Let your voice carry
intention, and let laughter, wit, and even a little
sacred gossip become medicine. It is OK to change
your mind. It is OK to hold two truths at once.

This card asks, Where are you being too rigid in
your thinking? Where can curiosity reopen the flow?

Every breath becomes an opportunity to connect
to others, to Spirit, and to the many mirrored selves
within you. Speak your truth. Ask the question. Follow
the thread. Gemini reminds you that communication
is not just a skill — it is a sacred path of awakening.

Gemini

May 21 - June 20

Shadow Path

When Gemini appears reversed, it may reveal mental overload, scattered thoughts, or a restless spirit spinning in too many directions. You may be caught in distraction loops, constantly shifting focus, or overconsuming information without integration.

Surface-level conversations, gossip, or avoidance through endless talking can leave you feeling ungrounded. There may be fear of choosing a single path or speaking a deeper truth. This dual-natured sign can become fragmented when it fears stillness, depth, or emotional exposure.

Say what is real. Reclaim your center. Breathe into your body. Be present. One honest conversation, spoken with clarity and care, can be a bridge back to yourself. Gemini reminds you that your truth has power when it is rooted in authenticity, not noise.

Symbolic Vision: Two mirrored figures sit cross-legged, cloaked in violet light — twin reflections of the same soul. Between their outstretched hands, a luminous dragonfly hovers with its wings refracting unseen frequencies. This sacred messenger flits between dimensions, carrying insight, memory, and revelation.

The dragonfly dances through timelines as easily as Gemini speaks between minds. Around them, orbs pulse with light and shadow, logic and imagination — reminders that duality is not a fracture, but a fluent exchange.

Gemini does not choose one path; it moves between them, curious and fluid, weaving contrast into coherence. The sky above swirls with shifting glyphs and symbols — codes of language, memory, and myth waiting for the right voice to unlock them. Gemini channels ideas into language and energy into story. It listens between the lines and translates the unseen. The voices you hear may not be your own — they could be echoes of other lives, timelines, or truths still unfolding.

Gemini is a conduit — a mystic scribe capturing change through words, laughter, and connection. Each thought, question, and breath of wonder becomes part of a living grimoire. This is not magic built on certainty but movement and meaning. Its power lies in paradox: the willingness to wonder, shift perspectives, and live in the question.

Gemini's astrological house — the third house of communication, intelligence, and early learning — pulses quietly in the background. It reminds us that language is not only a tool but also a transmission of Spirit. Through speech, we shape reality. Through listening, we heal. And through curiosity, we evolve.

The dragonfly does not fly in straight lines — it spirals, darts, and weaves through currents of possibility. So do you. Gemini teaches us that we are meant to be versatile, inquisitive, and willing to explore both sides of the story. Its air element infuses the mind with clarity and motion, but when scattered or overwhelmed, that air can become a storm of noise.

In shadow, the twins may fragment — lost in indecision, mental loops, or overstimulation. The invitation is to return to center, speak only what rings true, and honor communication as a sacred act. Your voice does not need to be the loudest, only the most aligned.

You are the translator of light. Your voice is a key. Speak truth, even as it evolves. Let your words become spells of illumination. Let your breath become a bridge between dimensions.

Sacred Reflection

What dualities exist within me, and how might they be working together? Rather than choosing one side, explore the space where both can be true. Your contradictions are bridges, not barriers — threads of thought and feeling woven into sacred coherence.

Ritual
Dual Sight and Sacred Dialogue

Supplies

- Two pieces of fabric in contrasting or complementary colors (light/dark, silver/gold)
- Needle and thread or fabric glue
- Natural stuffing such as cotton, dried herbs, or soft moss
- A parchment or strip of paper
- Optional symbols: Gemini glyph, Mercury sigil, dragonfly charm, or twin runes
- Gemini-aligned herbs, intuitively chosen: lavender (clarity), peppermint (activation), mugwort (intuition), chamomile (calm and softness)
- Crystals for Gemini's twin energies: blue lace agate (calms the mind and supports gentle, truthful communication) and citrine (activates curiosity, wit, and creative thinking while sparking joyful dialogue)

Step 1: Cast the Circle of Dialogue.

Begin by creating a sacred space. Light incense or ring wind chimes to invoke the air element. Say aloud, *"I open the space for truth to flow and for all my voices to find harmony. I call upon Mercury, air, and the whispering wind within me."* This begins the ritual of mirrored presence.

Step 2: Cut and Stitch the Twins Poppet.

Cut two identical pieces of fabric, each representing an aspect of the Gemini archetype. As you begin stitching the edges (leave space for stuffing), enter a breath-paced rhythm and whisper, *"With each stitch, I speak the spell. Two voices rise, one form to dwell. Thought and feeling, truth and dream, woven now in sacred seam."* And then repeat: *"With each stitch, I speak the spell."* When the poppet is nearly sealed, pause and whisper, *"One form, two faces. Two voices, one truth. May these twins know each other."*

Step 3: Fill with Breath and Memory.

Gently stuff the poppet with cotton or herbs. Speak first as your outer voice: *"I speak clarity, wit, and connection."* Then shift tone for the inner self: *"I carry dreams, whispers, and sacred wonder."* Tuck inside a parchment with a sigil or word of integration. Add blue lace agate to one side for calm, expressive truth. Add citrine to the other side to spark curiosity and illuminate intuitive thinking.

Step 4: Name the Twin Aspects.

Hold the poppet in your hands. Feel into each side's essence: solar and lunar, external and internal. Name them aloud: *"By breath and word, I name thee [name one] and [name two]. Speak through me as I speak for you."* You are now anchoring polarity into harmony.

Step 5: Draw or Embroider the Sigils.

Mark or adorn each side with a sacred symbol. Use what resonates: the Gemini glyph for dual unity, Mercury's sigil for movement and thought, a dragonfly for liminal messages, or a rune such as Ansuz for divine communication. These symbols serve as magical seals.

Step 6: Charge Under Wind and Word.

Place the poppet in moonlight or by an open window where the air can move freely. Say, *"Carry my thoughts through the ether. Let my voices merge and find harmony. In the spiral of breath and knowing, let clarity rise."* Optional: Write about this ritual in your Book of Shadows.

Step 7: Activate the Dialogue.

Use the poppet regularly. Journal from each voice. Pull cards for each twin. Whisper unsaid truths to it. Sleep with it near you during Mercury retrograde. Let it guide stories, channeled writing, and shadow healing. Close the ritual by holding the poppet in both hands and affirming, *"By thought and breath, by voice and wing, this poppet lives in sacred balance. So may it be."*

Element: Water

Ruling Planet: Moon

House: Fourth (family, emotions, home, subconscious self, domestic life)

Essence: *Lunar Wisdom ✦ Sacred Sensitivity ✦ Empathic Intuition ✦ Home and Hearth Magic*

Dragonfly Echo

I honor my emotions as sacred messengers. My softness is strength, and my boundaries are protection. I return to myself with compassion. It is safe to feel, rest, and choose peace. I nurture from fullness, not depletion. I am held, I am whole, and I am home.

25. Cancer: The Crab

Energetic Invitation: Cancer emerges from the tides of your inner world, inviting you into emotional presence and the sacred art of nurturing. The fourth sign of the zodiac, Cancer is ruled by the moon and aligned with the element of water — both symbols of intuition, rhythm, and reflection. This sign governs the fourth house in astrology, the realm of family, emotional roots, home, the subconscious, and the inner child.

When Cancer enters your field, you are being asked to soften, feel, and remember. Its shell may be protective, but beneath lies lunar wisdom and sacred sensitivity — gifts that guide you back to yourself.

This card invites you to tend to your inner sanctuary, your body, your home, and your breath. These are your altars. What emotional spaces need cleaning, nourishing, or honoring?

Cancer is the archetype of the mother, the empath, and the healer. Its magic is not loud; it whispers through intuition, memory, and mood. You are being encouraged to trust your empathic intuition, to retreat without shame, and to listen to what your emotional tides are trying to teach you. Your feelings are not distractions; they are sacred messengers leading you toward truth and integration.

This is a sign of strength wrapped in softness and of loyalty that protects like moonlit waves around the shore. Sometimes rest is not withdrawal — it is a warrior's pause. Protecting your peace is not passive; it is home and hearth magic in action.

Let yourself return. Let yourself feel. Let yourself be held by the moon, by water, and by you.

Cancer

June 21 - July 22

Shadow Path

Cancer's shadow may appear as overgiving, withdrawal, or emotional overwhelm.

Explore where you have abandoned your needs for others. Your sensitivity is strength, but only when held with boundaries.

Come home to yourself. Replenish. Reclaim your emotional sovereignty.

Where are you overextending emotionally? Is your shell protecting or isolating you?

Symbolic Vision: Swirled in the indigo currents of intuition and memory, the crab emerges—its spiral-patterned shell a sacred labyrinth of the soul. Cloaked in the iridescent glow of moonlit coral and ocean flame, this celestial creature carries the mysteries of the inner world across the tides of time.

The shell spirals inward like a glyph of ancient knowing, pulsing with the energy of remembrance. It is a living portal — a symbol of the subconscious and the sacred spiral of becoming.

Each claw curves in mirrored motion, forming twin crescents of protection and reception. These arcs embrace the emotional body, holding the heart space gently yet firmly. Here lies Cancer's gift: the power to hold space for grief and joy, memory and emotion, and silence and song. The crab reminds us that our softness is not weakness. Vulnerability is a sacred technology. Emotions are not chaos; they are currents of guidance and healing.

Ruled by the moon, Cancer channels the divine feminine in her most sacred form — fluid, reflective, and intuitive. The moon casts a silver light over the waters of the psyche, illuminating unseen truths and unlocking dreams. As it waxes and wanes, the moon teaches us that we also are ever-shifting and ever-becoming. Lunar wisdom flows through the shell and soul alike.

Aligned with the fourth house of astrology, Cancer governs the foundation of our emotional life: family, home, roots, and the sacred inner child. This house is the dwelling of soul memory. It is where we carry our lineage, our mother line, and our ancestral waters. Cancer calls us to tend to this space, nourish it, and build sanctuary not just in physical spaces but also within our bodies and breath.

The Crab's legs stir the spiraling waters below, echoing the rhythm of the moon's pull — ebbing and flowing, retreating and returning. This rhythm is not passive; it is intelligent and deeply attuned. Cancer moves sideways, not out of fear but as an act of instinctual protection and intuitive timing. It teaches us that not all paths are linear. Sometimes we spiral inward to heal. Sometimes retreat is sacred strategy.

Cancer is the guardian of the inner temple and the protector of hearth and heart. It whispers, *"You are both the shell and the soul within it."* You are the vessel and the ocean. Your sensitivity is your strength. Your emotional wisdom is your spell. You carry the tides within you — and your magic is made of memory, moonlight, and deep feeling made holy.

Sacred Reflection

What does emotional safety feel like, and where do I most need it now? Turn inward. Name the spaces, relationships, or rituals that help you feel held. Let this clarity reveal where you need softness and where sacred boundaries restore your inner sanctuary.

Ritual

Moon Mirror of Inner Knowing

- A clear glass or silver bowl or any vessel that feels sacred
- Moon-charged water or fresh water available to you
- Crystals: moonstone for intuition and divine feminine flow, selenite for energetic purification and protection (do not submerge), and aquamarine to soothe the heart and bring emotional clarity
- A white or blue cloth or silk scarf (optional)
- Access to moonlight, either outdoors or through a window
- Herbal infusion or mojo bag with chamomile (soothe), motherwort (steady), marshmallow root (soften), skullcap (quiet), or milky oats (nourish)

Step 1: Prepare the Waters.

Fill your sacred bowl with water, and place it on a white or blue cloth under moonlight. Whisper into the bowl with reverence, *"Luna of the sea and sky, shine through this sacred mirror. Reveal what the soul is ready to receive."*

Place your moonstone or aquamarine in the water if water-safe. Keep your selenite nearby to bless and guard the space.

Step 2: Anoint with Herbs.

Create a soothing tea or mojo bag using the listed herbs. Slowly sip the tea or rest the sachet near your bowl. Let your body soften and your nervous system settle. The herbs open you to the quiet pulse of lunar wisdom.

Step 3: Align with Crystals.

Hold the moonstone at your heart or womb space ,and breathe deeply. Feel its intuitive rhythm match your own. Gently place aquamarine in the bowl or in front of it. Let it wash your emotions with calm clarity. Place selenite near the water's edge to hold protective space and keep your channel clear.

Step 4: Meditate While Moon-Gazing.

Sit quietly, and gaze at the water's surface. Let the moonlight shimmer across the bowl. Don't seek visions; simply witness. Let colors, emotions, memories, or intuitive sparks emerge in their own time.

Step 5: Channel the Message.

When something stirs within, speak aloud or whisper what you feel, see, or hear. Let your voice move like water: fluid, intuitive, and gentle. Write down everything you receive in a sacred journal or moon diary.

Step 6: Seal the Portal.

Place your hands above the bowl. Thank the moon, the water, your guides, and yourself. Imagine the bowl sealing with a soft silver veil. Offer the water to the earth or a plant, returning vision to the soil.

Step 7: Integrate with Moonstone.

Before bed, hold your moonstone agaim. Imagine the water's light glowing inside you — quiet, sacred, and wise. Whisper, *"What was seen flows inward.What was heard echoes in silence. I trust the tides of knowing."*

Element: Fire

Ruling Planet: Sun

House: Fifth (creativity, romance, risk, children)

Essence: *Confident ✦ Magnetism ✦ Self-Expression ✦ Boastful ✦ Accepting ✦ Bubbly*

Dragonfly Echo

I am confident and radiant. I express my truth with courage and creativity. My self-expression flows freely: bubbly, bold, and accepting of every facet of my being. I do not shrink; I shine. Even when others misunderstand me, I trust my light. I am brave, boastful, and beautifully aligned.

26. Leo: The Lion

Energetic Invitation: You are the radiant sovereign of fire. Leo bursts into your reading like a solar flare — warm, unapologetic, and divinely magnetic. As the fifth sign of the zodiac, Leo is ruled by the sun, the golden source of light, life, and creative fire. This card invites you into your fullest self-expression: bold, courageous, and fiercely authentic. You are not here to hide; you are here to shine.

Leo is the sacred performer, the creative leader, and the guardian of heart-centered confidence. When this archetype rises, it is a call to take up space with pride. Be boastful in your brilliance — not from ego, but from reverence.

Leo reminds you that your joy, your voice, and your story are sacred. Every laugh, every gesture, and every burst of creative fire is an offering to the world. Your self-expression is a divine spark in motion.

You are not too much — you are the sun. Your energy was born to inspire. Let your confidence be a blessing. Let your charisma ripple outward, igniting others through your presence. Even your bubbly joy has healing power.

Leo calls you to center your inner child, celebrate your gifts, and lead with love. You do not have to seek permission to radiate. The sun does not ask to rise. It simply shines.

Now is the time to dance in your light. Trust the pulse of passion within you. Be beautifully aligned with your truth, and let your heart blaze its sacred fire across every part of your path.

Leo

July 23 - August 22

Boastful • Accepting • Bubbly
Confident • Magnetism • Self-Expression

July 23 - August 22

♌

Leo

☉

The Lion

26

Shadow Path

When Leo appears reversed, the radiant flame dims. Insecurity may show up as boastfulness or exaggerated charm.

You might crave attention — not from joy, but from fear, performing for validation rather than expressing your truth. Maybe you are shrinking to avoid judgment or inflating your presence to be seen. Both responses pull you away from your inner sun.

This is your call to return to the light within. You do not need applause or perfection to be worthy. Love is not earned by performance — it is your birthright. Let your self-expression arise from soul, not from the hunger to be noticed. Reclaim your joy for yourself. Your courage is real when rooted in truth. Let the sun warm you from within. Shine for alignment, not approval.

Symbolic Vision: Against a fiery backdrop of solar gold and red, the lion gazes forward — regal, calm, and unshaken. Its eyes burn with the steady power of self-awareness, courage, and pride.

Its mane, luminous and wild, flares like a living crown of flame — part constellation, part auric field, and part eternal blaze. It radiates outward in waves, echoing Leo's signature essence: confidence, magnetism, and self-expression.

Above the lion's head glows the glyph of the sun, Leo's ruling planet and the beating heart of the cosmos. Here the sun is not simply a celestial body — it is the sacred fire of the soul. Through Leo, the sun learns how to shine with presence and joy. This is the archetype of solar sovereignty:

the one who creates not to perform, but to illuminate. The lion's gift is this unwavering authenticity — being wholly oneself with nothing to prove.

Each strand of the mane becomes a golden thread connecting Leo to the divine spark. Within this blaze lies the fifth house of astrology: the realm of romance, creativity, children, play, and passion. This is the house of joy as a sacred ritual. The inner child is alive here, dancing in full color, daring you to take risks, be bold, and lead with heart instead of fear.

Leo teaches that playfulness is medicine and that vulnerability, when rooted in joy, is powerful. The lion does not roar to be heard. It roars because its soul cannot be silenced. Whether through song, dance, storytelling, or bold fashion, Leo shows us how to transform presence into art.

Its shadow may tempt with boastful pride, but at its core Leo does not crave a spotlight for attention. It shines because its truth is light. The solar glyph above the lion's head reflects a truth from within: You are the sun. You are the spark that begins the story, the warmth that sustains it, and the courage that completes it.

Surrounding the lion are golden flames shaped like hearts and stars — symbols of love, radiance, and the fearless expression of soul. Every pulse in this scene invites you to ignite your creative fire — not to impress, but to inspire.

You are the sovereign flame, a radiant presence born to illuminate. Your joy becomes your magnetism, drawing others toward the warmth of your authenticity. Your courage is not a performance; it is your sacred magic.

The light you carry doesn't just shine; it guides. It leads others home to their own brilliance. You were never meant to dim. You were always meant to blaze — wild, golden, and unapologetically whole.

Sacred Reflection

What part of me deserves a crown but has been waiting for someone else to place it? Where have you been withholding self-recognition? What talent, trait, or passion are you waiting to have validated? Celebrate your sovereign power without waiting for permission.

Ritual

Radiant Muse

Supplies

- Art supplies (markers, paints, collage materials, or colored pencils)
- A playlist of music that makes you feel confident, fierce, or joyful
- A journal or sketchbook
- Something gold, red, bold, or dramatic to wear
- A candle (gold, orange, or red)
- A bowl, cauldron, or other fire-safe container
- A drawn or printed sun symbol or Leo glyph

Step 1: Light the Flame of the Muse.

Dress in something bold — your favorite gold jewelry, sun-kissed tones, or an outfit that makes you feel like royalty. Adorn your space with symbols of Leo: sun glyphs, sunflowers, lions, or solar imagery. Light a candle with reverence, and place it at the center of your altar. As the flame flickers, breathe in its radiance and declare, *"I welcome the fire of inspiration. I call upon the sun to awaken the brilliance of my soul. My happiness is sacred. My creativity is a flame that never dies."* Let this be your sacred ignition.

Step 2: Dance with the Fire.

Play music that makes your body want to move. Begin gently, and then let the rhythm rise. Stomp to release fear, sway to awaken grace, and spin to stir joy. Use your body as a wand, channeling your emotions into movement. Say, *"I move with courage. I move with pleasure. I am the flame, fierce and alive."* Let every gesture affirm your wild vitality.

Step 3: Create Your Fire Print.

Gather paints, pastels, markers, or collage pieces. Let your hands move freely with no goal but expression. Layer, splash, or scribble — this is your soul's heat on paper. Title your creation something royal, such as "Sovereign Spark" or "Radiant Pulse." Let this visual piece become a symbol of your uninhibited inner fire.

Step 4: Speak the Candlelit Confidence Spell.

Sit before your flame. Let it reflect in your eyes and heart. Speak into the light, *"I am lit from within. My fire is fearless. My voice matters. My joy creates worlds."*

Hold your hands near the warmth, and envision the flame igniting your solar plexus. Feel your courage pulse brighter. Feel yourself rise.

Step 5: Write a Love Letter.

Write freely in your journal. Celebrate your voice, creativity, and presence. Begin with, *"Dear Radiant Flame, I celebrate you when...."*

Honor the parts of you that dare to be seen and heard. Let this letter be your reminder that self-love is sacred fire.

Step 6: Burn the Block, and Feed the Flame.

Write down a fear, judgment, or false story that dims your shine. Safely burn it in a fire-safe bowl. As the smoke rises say, *"My fire is stronger than fear. I release what dims my joy. I am here to shine."*

Watch the paper transform to ash. Feel the release.

Step 7: Seal with Solar Gratitude.

Place your hands on your heart. Breathe in the warmth you have summoned. Gaze at the candle and say, *"I am the artist. I am the flame. I am the joy. I shine from the inside out."*

Slowly blow out the candle, letting the smoke carry your spell of radiant becoming into the ethers.

Element: Earth

Ruling Planet: Mercury

House: Sixth (healing, work, service, health)

Essence: *Knowledgeable ✦ Sympathetic ✦ Service ✦ Attractive ✦ Practical ✦ Organized ✦ Anxious ✦ Ritual*

Dragonfly Echo

I trust in my ability to bring order, healing, and balance into my life. I honor the small, practical steps that lead to great results. My devotion to the details becomes a sacred act of alignment, clarity, and care that I implement daily.

27. Virgo: The Virgin

Energetic Invitation: When Virgo graces your path, you are being called into a season of sacred refinement — an invitation to clear space, ground into truth, and lovingly tend to your daily rituals. This is not about perfection; it is about presence.

Virgo's energy is ruled by Mercury and aligned with the sixth house of healing, health, service, and daily rhythm. You are stepping into a cycle where your devotion becomes your magic.

You are the quiet force that sees what others miss. Your organized mind, thoughtful nature, and capacity for discernment are not just skills — they are medicine. You are deeply sympathetic and practical, knowing how to nurture others with care that is both beautiful and useful.

This moment asks you to apply that same attention inward. What needs adjusting? What feels off-center? Your systems, routines, and rituals are sacred scaffolding, each one supporting the bloom of your well-being.

Virgo energy thrives in simplicity, natural beauty, and gentle service. It whispers that you don't have to save the world, just honor the parts of you that are already whole. Light a candle with purpose. Make a list with heart. Brew tea as an offering to your nervous system. Speak gently to your body, and listen when it speaks back.

You are the healer and the healed. You are both the medicine and the method. Let your sacred yes guide each task, and trust that your practicality and presence are enough. This isn't about doing more. It's about doing what matters with devotion.

Virgo

August 23 - September 22

Shadow Path

When Virgo energy tilts into shadow, you may feel overly anxious, hypercritical, or caught in loops of self-improvement. Perfectionism becomes a prison, and your sacred desire to serve can turn into overfunctioning or martyrdom. You may become consumed by the details and lose sight of the bigger picture or believe that worth must be earned through output and doing.

This card asks you to soften. Let go of the need to get it all right. There is no prize for perfection, only exhaustion. Your rituals are meant to restore, not restrict. Your systems are meant to support, not suffocate. Beware of weaponizing your wisdom against yourself. You are not broken. You are blooming — imperfectly, exquisitely, and in divine order.

Symbolic Vision: Amid a field of emerald light and swirling orbs, the figure of the virgin stands in quiet power, with her gaze focused and her presence anchored in clarity.

A crown of sacred geometry rests upon her brow, while her hair is intricately braided, each twist an offering to mindfulness and intention. She is composed but never cold. There is warmth in her stillness and intelligence in her care.

At her heart the Virgo glyph glows softly, pulsing like a mantra of devotion. It is not a symbol of judgment but of discernment — a beacon that calls forth the highest within the mundane. Behind her the Virgo constellation gleams like a sacred pattern, reminding us that even in chaos there is order waiting to be revealed.

Virgo is the guardian of the sixth house, the realm of healing, wellness, work, and conscious service. She teaches us that our routines are not meaningless repetitions but containers for transformation. She whispers that health — whether physical, emotional, or mental — is an ecosystem to be nurtured. The simplest acts of care are sacred when done with presence.

Her planetary ruler, Mercury, flows through her not as speed or speech, but as clear thought, refined expression, and deep analysis. Through Mercury's wisdom, Virgo becomes the sacred steward — tending, assessing, and elevating each detail into meaning. There is magic in the way she folds laundry, brews herbal tea, or organizes a cluttered shelf. Her practicality is a prayer. Her organization is an artform. She heals not with fanfare but with faithfulness.

Ruled by the element of earth, Virgo connects us to the tangible. She reminds us that ritual lives in what we touch, taste, and tend. Her knowledgeable nature is grounded in observation. She is deeply sympathetic and never loses herself in others. Her gift of service is wise, not self-sacrificing.

Virgo doesn't demand perfection; she honors wholeness. Her strength is in recognizing what needs clearing, what needs softening, and what deserves celebration. She brings light to what others ignore and beauty to what others rush past. She is the flame keeper of sacred space, both internal and external.

Even when she feels anxious, Virgo reaches for her tools — lists, breathwork, and grounding rituals — not to control, but to return. In her world, ritual is not an escape; it is a path home.

Virgo is the devoted one and the quiet architect of renewal. She invites you to become your own caretaker and to treat your body like a temple, your habits like altars, and your life like a garden that blooms with your noticing. You are not here to fix yourself; you are here to faithfully tend to your sacred becoming.

Sacred Reflection

What does sacred service mean to me, and how am I embodying it? Service becomes sacred when rooted in presence and purpose. Consider where your service uplifts and depletes. How can you honor yourself when showing up for others?

Ritual

Sacred Devotion and Refinement

Supplies

- Small broom or cleansing tool for sweeping energy
- Herbal tea: lemon balm, chamomile, mint, or lavender
- White or earth-toned cloth
- Bowl of warm water with a few drops of essential oil
- A candle (green, white, or brown)
- A crystal: amazonite (clarity, organization, and boundaries), moss agate (vitality and connection to nature), or fluorite (enhances focus and neutralizes overthinking)

Step 1: Prepare the Temple.

With intention, lay your cloth across a surface. Arrange your tools as if creating a miniature altar. Light your candle and softly say, *"This is my sacred space. This is my sacred time. I am the one who tends the altar of the everyday."* Sweep the space, allowing stagnant energy to drift away. Imagine a spiral of emerald-green light washing through the room.

Step 2: Invoke Virgo.

Place both hands over your heart, and anchor into stillness. Say aloud, *"Virgo, keeper of sacred order, vessel of wisdom and devotion, walk with me now. Show me what needs tending. Help me become the prayer, the pattern, and the peace."* Let your breath steady. Feel Virgo's essence arrive softly, clearly, and quietly powerful.

Step 3: Sip Ritual Tea as Medicine.

Sip your tea with deep presence. As the warmth fills you say, *"I take in calm. I take in care. I take in grace."* With each sip, imagine your nervous system smoothing and your thoughts organizing themselves into clarity.

Step 4: Wash Your Hands with Devotion.

Dip your fingers into the bowl of warm, scented water. As you wash your hands say, *"These hands create my life. They heal, they serve, and they organize beauty into form. May all I touch today be touched with love."* Move slowly. Feel every motion as prayer.

Step 5: Whisper the Refinement.

Close your eyes, and name aloud three things you are ready to release, such as mental clutter, criticism, or overscheduling. Then name three supportive practices you will carry forward. And then say, *"I release what binds me. I embrace what nourishes me."* Visualize these intentions flowing into your chosen crystal.

Step 6: Charge the Crystal.

Hold your amazonite, moss agate, or fluorite crystal to your heart and say, *"I call in discernment, not judgment. I call in structure, not pressure. I call in healing, not haste."*

Let it absorb your intention. Keep the crystal close as a guide throughout your week.

Step 7: Close the Circle.

Blow out the candle with reverence and say, *"This ritual continues in how I live and in how I clean, nourish, serve, and speak. I am the healer. I am the vessel. I am the devotion."*

Place your hands in prayer or gently over your solar plexus. Breathe deeply, anchoring this sacred frequency into your body.

Element: Air

Ruling Planet: Venus

House: Seventh (relationships, including partner/marriage, lovers, business, collaboration)

Essence: *Balanced ✦ Harmony ✦ Conscious Choice ✦ Captivating ✦ Indecisive ✦ Justice ✦ Beauty*

Dragonfly Echo

I am the sacred alchemist of harmony. I stir the unseen, blend opposites, and return to balance. I honor beauty, truth, and relational wisdom. I choose grace with power, silence with purpose, and justice with love. I recalibrate with intention. I am peace in motion. I am equilibrium made sacred.

28. Libra: The Cauldrons

Energetic Invitation: You are the sacred alchemist of harmony. Libra, the seventh sign of the zodiac, arrives with an invitation to recalibrate your life through intentional beauty, conscious balance, and relational grace. Symbolized by the cauldrons, not just scales, Libra brews stillness and movement, assertion and receptivity, and silence and song into a sacred equilibrium. This is not passive neutrality but the fierce artistry of alignment.

Ruled by Venus, the goddess of love and aesthetics, and aligned with the air element, Libra brings refinement to the emotional and intellectual realms. Here, beauty is not decoration; it is a form of sacred justice. Grace is not weakness; it is wisdom in motion. Libra teaches that harmony is created, not inherited, and must include both self and others.

The seventh house governs partnerships, soul contracts, lovers, and conscious collaborations. This is the realm of mirror magic, where your relationships reflect the energy you cultivate within. If your inner scales feel tipped, tune in. What is unspoken that needs voice? What needs boundaries? What longs to be seen?

You are being asked to stir your cauldron, harmonize the dissonant, soften control, and assert with compassion. Even indecision holds power when met with awareness.

Let your breath become balance. Let your life become a poem of beauty and justice. Libra is not just the peacekeeper—it is the conscious chooser, the graceful warrior, and the divine mirror of what's possible when we live in truth and trust.

Libra

September 23 - October 22

Shadow Path

When Libra appears reversed, the cauldrons of harmony may be tipping out of alignment. This shadow speaks to a disconnection from your inner truth: a pattern of conflict avoidance, people-pleasing, or prioritizing surface-level beauty at the expense of deeper balance.

You may be holding back your authentic voice to keep the peace, allowing resentment or fatigue to build. Libra's shadow is not chaos; it is the illusion of harmony masking internal dissonance.

This is your invitation to pause and realign. Where are you afraid to disrupt the calm,? Where have you been indecisive to avoid disappointing others? The sacred path of Libra asks not for perfection, but for conscious recalibration.

Symbolic Vision: Suspended in a violet field of twilight magic, two radiant cauldrons hover midair—perfectly poised in mirrored tension, like the sacred scales that govern the Libran soul.

Between them, spirals of flame rise in hues of indigo, rose, and gold, neither fire overpowering the other. These are not reckless fires but deliberate, alchemical flames. They symbolize the soul's yearning for equilibrium, where beauty is born from balance and truth emerges from stillness.

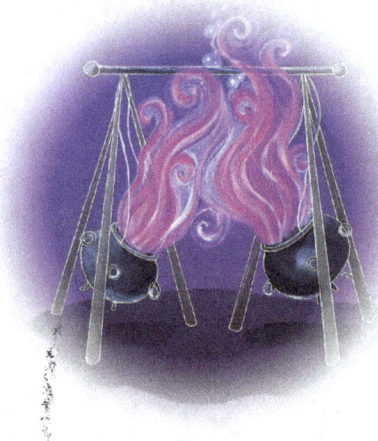

Each cauldron glows with its own pulse, shimmering in cosmic rhythm. They hold potential and presence, not resolution. Together they embody the heart of Libra's sacred practice: conscious choice. This energy teaches us that balance is not about neutrality or avoidance — it is the intentional act of holding contradiction, weighing all possibilities with grace. Every pause before action, every breath before a word, is part of the spell of harmony being cast.

Above, the glyph of Venus — the planet of beauty, magnetism, and love — shines

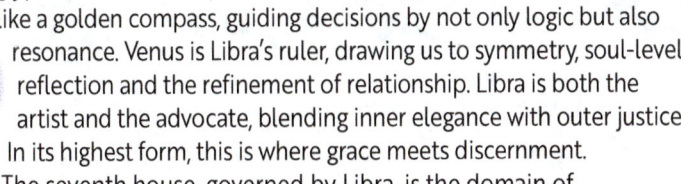

like a golden compass, guiding decisions by not only logic but also resonance. Venus is Libra's ruler, drawing us to symmetry, soul-level reflection and the refinement of relationship. Libra is both the artist and the advocate, blending inner elegance with outer justice. In its highest form, this is where grace meets discernment.

The seventh house, governed by Libra, is the domain of partnerships: romantic, platonic, professional, and spiritual. It is the mirror through which we meet ourselves in the presence of another. This is not always easy. Libra energy may struggle with indecision, people-pleasing, or suppressing conflict to maintain peace. But true harmony does not come from suppression; it comes from presence, showing up with your full self and trusting the beauty of authenticity.

The cauldrons glisten with an almost musical vibration, offering a message: You are the sacred alchemist of your own life. Balance is not about perfection. It is about rhythm. The flame that rises must also soften. The voice that speaks must also listen. Justice lives not in force but in embodied fairness. Artistry lives in the choices you make with care.

Libra's symbolic vision invites you to make your life a cauldron, blending emotion and logic, grace and power, and vulnerability and strength. Let beauty be your inner barometer. Let alignment be your aim. Let every relationship you engage in — whether with a person, a dream, or your own reflection — be a vessel of awareness.

Let the cauldrons sway but never shatter. Let the sacred flame burn steady. Let your every step be a dance of harmony in motion.

Sacred Reflection

What feels out of balance in my life right now, and what part of me needs to be heard more deeply? Let your inner scales speak. Explore where you are overextending, receiving too little, or silencing your truth in the name of harmony. What needs a voice?

Ritual
Relationship Clarity

Supplies

- *A small scale (symbolic or real, or you can use two balanced fire-safe bowls or cauldrons)*
- *Incense (rose, sandalwood, frankincense, or lavender)*
- *Dried herbs or petals for burning (optional: rose petals, bay leaf, rosemary)*
- *A lighter or matches*
- *Paper and pen*
- *A Venus or Libra symbol (drawn or placed nearby)*

Step 1: Set the Altar of Balance

Place your scale at the center of your altar. Set the two cauldrons or fire-safe bowls on either side — representing "Self" and "Other." Light your incense and say aloud, *"I invoke the energy of Libra, the weaver of balance, harmony, and beauty. May smoke reveal the truth that silence hides. May clarity rise."*

Step 2: Name the Relationship.

Write the name of the person or relationship around which you seek clarity on a small piece of paper. Fold it once, and place it gently beneath the incense holder. Say, *"This connection is worthy of reflection. I open my heart to see what is unseen."*

Step 3: Weigh the Heart and Mind.

Sit quietly before the scale and reflect: *"What does this relationship bring me? What does it cost me? What is being exchanged, and is it equal?"* In your journal, write one truth for the heart (emotion) and one for the mind (logic). Place the heart truth in the left bowl and the mind truth in the right one. These become the symbolic weights of your inner scale.

Step 4: Burn the Illusions.

Choose one belief, expectation, or old narrative that clouds your clarity. Write it on a small slip of paper. Burn it in one of the cauldrons while saying, *"I release the story that no longer serves truth. May smoke clear what fear conceals."* Watch the smoke rise, and visualize false beliefs dissolving.

Step 5: Invoke the Mirror of Venus.

Waft the incense smoke toward your face and chest. Hold your palms open as if holding a mirror and say aloud, *"I see clearly. I love wisely. I balance with grace. Through Venus, I choose connection without losing myself."* Let the fragrance fill your lungs and soften your heart.

Step 6: Rebalance the Scales.

Take one petal, herb, or token and place it in each cauldron, symbolizing equal exchange. Say, *"I give and receive in balance. I honor both my needs and theirs. I choose relationships that reflect mutual devotion and truth."* If one side still feels heavier, ask yourself what needs to shift for equilibrium?

Step 7: Seal with Smoke and Choice.

Hold the incense again, and draw the smoke in a figure-eight or infinity symbol in front of you. Say aloud, *"I walk in balance. I love with discernment. I release what is unclear. I call in aligned connection."* Let the incense burn to completion. Scatter the ashes outside or into running water as an offering to air and flow.

Element: Water

Ruling Planet: Pluto (modern), Mars (traditional)

House: Eighth (death, transformation, deep bonds)

Essence: *Karma ✦ Death and Rebirth ✦ Intense ✦ Release ✦ Sexuality ✦ Jealousy ✦ Mystery*

Dragonfly Echo

I shed what no longer serves my soul and rise in my empowered truth. I honor the shadows as sacred teachers and trust the depth of my intelligence. My sexuality is sacred, my mind is sharp, and my transformation is unstoppable.

29. Scorpio: The Scorpion

Energetic Invitation: Scorpio arrives when your soul is ready for alchemy. As the eighth sign of the zodiac, Scorpio rules the eighth house of deep bonds, soul contracts, karma, and transformation.

Governed by Mars in ancient astrology and Pluto in modern tradition, Scorpio is aligned with fierce evolution through intimacy, shadow, mystery, and release.

When this card enters your field, you are not being asked to stay comfortable. You are being invited into the sacred descent. Something within or around you is dissolving, dying, or shedding — and though this may stir fear or resistance, it is sacred.

Endings hold the wisdom of beginnings. Death clears the way for rebirth. Trust that what is leaving cannot hold your future and what rises from these ashes will be more aligned, resilient, and radiant.

This invitation asks you to stop hiding your emotional truth. The things you have buried — fears, jealousies, desires, and shame — are not weaknesses but initiations. Let what you have kept secret be witnessed in safe, sacred space. Scorpio teaches us that the very poison we fear can become the potion that heals if we hold it with consciousness.

Examine where you are clinging to control or resisting the cycle of death and rebirth. The mystery is not to be solved; it is to be surrendered to. This is your rite of passage. Let the old fall away. Let transformation take root. You are not breaking — you are becoming. And every time you emerge, you come back more whole.

♏ Scorpio ♂

October 23 - November 21

Shadow Path

When Scorpio appears reversed or in shadow, it may signal resistance to change, emotional suppression, or power struggles cloaked in secrecy. You might be clinging to what no longer serves out of fear and avoiding the transformation that could liberate you.

Jealousy, manipulation, or obsession may rise, asking to be healed. Are you withholding truth, using silence as control, or hiding wounds behind a façade of power?

Scorpio's shadows are intense because its medicine is profound. When you suppress pain, it festers. When you fear endings, you block rebirth. Where you are resisting emotional depth, avoiding vulnerability, or fearing your own intensity? Transformation begins where you stop pretending.

Symbolic Vision: In the deepest waters, where silence presses and shadows whisper, Scorpio finds sanctuary. It does not fear the dark—it becomes it.

Suspended in this subterranean world, the scorpion rules with an unseen strength. It is not chaos that dwells here but alchemy. This is not stillness that weakens but stillness that transforms.

The scorpion, fierce yet refined, symbolizes Scorpio's sacred instinct to protect, perceive, and transform. Its exoskeleton reflects your emotional armor, while its sting holds the power of sacred boundaries and truth-telling.

It is nocturnal for a reason — its magic unfolds in the mystery. In every crevice of the unseen world, Scorpio is alive, sensing what others miss. This is the realm of secrets, sex, and surrender, and of karmic ties and soul contracts.

The swirling waters behind the scorpion pulse with the weight of inheritance and emotional depth. Here lies the realm of the eighth house, where legacy, power, intimacy, death, and rebirth reside.

Scorpio invites you into sacred surrender, releasing control and allowing metamorphosis. Not everything must be solved. Some things must be alchemized.

Pluto, Scorpio's modern ruler, brings the transformative flames of rebirth. Mars, its ancient ruler, infuses you with courage to walk into the storm. Together they guide the soul through cycles of karmic unraveling and empowered return.

Scorpio governs this sacred threshold between what was and what will be. Your current transformation may feel like death, but it is a portal to the most authentic version of your being.

Let the mystery nourish you. Let jealousy become inquiry. Let desire become soul movement. Let release open the gates to liberation. Let sexuality become ritual. You are the phoenix and the flame, the sacred storm and the sacred stillness.

This is not surface magic. It is root-deep resurrection.

Sacred Reflection

How do I protect my emotional energy, and is it still serving me? Scorpio's armor guards the softest soul. Examine your emotional boundaries. Are they rigid, fluid, absent? When and why did you build them? What would it feel like to allow vulnerability?

Ritual

Baptism of the Shadow

Supplies

- A black or violet candle
- A bowl of still water (moon-charged or spring water, if available)
- Essential oil: myrrh, patchouli, or ylang-ylang
- Crystal: obsidian, labradorite, or carnelian
- A mirror (handheld or altar-based)
- A strip of paper and pen
- Optional: Red wine or pomegranate juice for offering

Step 1: Prepare the Portal.

This ritual is designed to be performed in the shower or bath, where water becomes the sacred medium of release, purification, and spiritual resurrection. Guided by the archetype of the water scorpion, you will descend into your emotional depths, shed what no longer serves you, and rise reborn in sovereignty and sacred power.

Light the black or violet candle beside your water bowl. Anoint your heart, navel, and third eye with a drop of oil. Hold your crystal to your third eye and say aloud, *"By shadow and flame, by still water and soul, I call forth the sacred rite of rebirth."*

Step 2: Enter the Waters.

Step into your bath or shower. Let the water run over your body. Say with authority, *"I descend willingly into my depths. I am not afraid of my shadow. I am here to transform."* As water touches you, imagine old stories, soul contracts, and emotional debris being washed away.

Step 3: Shadow Gaze

Step from the water and look into the mirror. Gaze deeply into your own eyes and say, *"I see the one who survived. I see the one who still rises."* Hold your crystal while observing your reflection. Notice any emotions that rise, and let them be felt, not judged.

Step 4: Name What Must Die.

On a strip of paper, write down a pattern, wound, belief, or energetic tie that must be surrendered. Say, *"This is the old skin. This no longer belongs to me."* Place the paper beneath your bowl of water as a symbolic drowning of the past.

Step 5: Purify and Release.

Retrieve the paper. Either burn it in the candle flame (safely), or tear and dissolve it in your bowl of water. Say, *"By fire or by flood, I dissolve the tie. Let it die. Let it go."* Pour the water into the earth or down the drain, releasing with reverence.

Step 6: Reclaim the Soul.

Hold your crystal at your solar plexus or womb. Say, *"I call back my energy, my wisdom, and my fire. I reclaim what was lost and awaken what was hidden."* Dab oil again at your temples and wrists. Envision a radiant version of you emerging from still water, crowned in sovereignty.

Step 7: Seal the Rite with Offering.

Offer a sip of red wine or pomegranate juice to the earth, your altar, or simply raise it in gratitude. Say these final words, *"I have died, and I have risen. I walk now in truth, intimacy, and sacred power. So it is."* Snuff the candle, breathe deeply, and allow integration.

Element: Fire

Ruling Planet: Jupiter

House: Ninth (philosophy, higher learning, and long-distance journeys)

Essence: Masculine: *Freedom ✦ Teacher ✦ Philosophy ✦ Exploration ✦ Divine Desire ✦ Optimism* Feminine: *Adventure ✦ Seeker ✦ Visionary Path ✦ Boundless ✦ Quest ✦ Luck ✦ Erotic Desire*

Dragonfly Echo

I trust my longing, my body's wisdom, and my fire of adventure. My truth is my compass. I follow joy, explore boldly, and believe in magic. I am the flame of freedom, guided by curiosity, ignited by expansion, and destined for more.

30. Sagittarius: The Centaur

Energetic Invitation: Sagittarius arrives like a blazing gust of wind and is like a spark that refuses to be caged. Ruled by Jupiter — the great planet of expansion, wisdom, and divine luck — Sagittarius the ninth sign of the zodiac. Its energy urges you to seek, soar, and say yes to the unknown.

Sagittarians do not follow tradition for comfort; they follow instinct for truth. This is the path of the seeker, the philosopher, and the ecstatic wanderer whose altar is the open road and whose devotion is experience itself.

The centaur embodies this sacred duality — hoofed in the earth, yet arrowed to the stars. It teaches that we are both human and divine, wild and wise, grounded and visionary. You are now being invited to stretch your beliefs, leap into the mystery, and trust your body's desire for liberation. You are not escaping; you are remembering.

Whether through study, sacred sexuality, pilgrimage, poetry, movement, or meaningful dialogue, your soul longs to be lit with new meaning. The adventure ahead is not about a destination — it's about rediscovering the fire of your becoming. Trust that your pleasure is a compass. Let curiosity be your teacher. Say yes even if you don't know where it will lead.

This is your sacred permission slip to leap. Start the class. Begin the manuscript. Take the trip. Explore the edges of your comfort. The sacred arrow you carry is blessed with purpose. Let it fly beyond fear. Let it land in freedom. Let it lead you back home to yourself. You are the sacred explorer of truths.

✗ Sagittarius ♃

November 22 – December 21

Shadow Path

When Sagittarius appears reversed, its flame may flicker into restlessness or rebellion. The sacred quest becomes an escape route, and the arrow aims without intention.

You may feel untethered — chasing novelty, romanticizing distant horizons, or overindulging in movement without integration. There can be a tendency to bypass discomfort, mistaking change for progress and distraction for growth. Are you running toward freedom or away from truth? Are you truly exploring or avoiding embodiment?

When the centaur turns from the path of meaning, expansion becomes scattering. Authentic growth requires both motion and reflection. It's time to pause and root into presence. Let your desire return to its sacred center. Let truth, not urgency, lead.

Symbolic Vision: Masculine

Sagittarius emerges in silhouette, with tribal spirals dancing across his body like sacred maps of fire-born truth. With his bow drawn beneath Jupiter's golden blaze, he gallops through realms unseen — freedom igniting every stride. His form is wild and divine, strength braided with vision.

A teacher in motion, he rides not for escape but revelation. Fire fuels his purpose, and luck rides beside him whispering, *"Expand. Become."*

The solar glow behind him echoes the light he carries — a beacon of bold philosophy and sacred optimism. This is not just a chase; it is a pilgrimage of mind, body, and spirit.

You are the wisdom in motion. Let your thoughts soar like arrows.

A radiant blaze roars behind the **feminine Sagittarius**, but she does not flinch. The centauride rides through flame, with her bow lifted toward the unseen horizon. Her body is a living myth that moves with erotic freedom and fierce

purpose. Every muscle hums with questing; every flicker of her mane catches the light of destiny. She is not chasing places; she's following a vision. She spirals through dimensions where fire speaks in symbols and truth is sacred terrain. Her power is not in taming; it is in traveling, asking, and opening. Luck loves her because she dares to leap.

You are the seeker on fire — ride the edge, and let desire be your compass.

Combined symbolism: Under the blazing glow of Jupiter's golden gaze, Sagittarius gallops into the unknown — half wild, half divine. The centaur and centauride rise as mirrored flames: one tribal and shadowed, and the other pale and luminous, both archers of destiny. Their arrows are questions. Their hooves spark meaning.

Fire is their element — alive, boundless, and transformative. It does not destroy; it liberates. Fueled by erotic desire, sacred philosophy, and raw instinct, they chase the visionary path, where knowledge is earned through motion.

Jupiter, planet of luck, governs this sign, gifting synchronicity and expansion to those who dare. Sagittarius rules the ninth house, where higher learning, long-distance travel, and spiritual exploration converge.

Freedom is not a luxury; it is the essence. Optimism is not naive; it is cosmic. To walk the Sagittarian path is to leap into experience and to quest for truth with a heart lit by stars.

This archetype teaches that to seek is to awaken, that wisdom lives in the untraveled road, and that desire — when aligned with spirit — is divine. You are the adventure, the teacher, and the spark that will not be tamed. Let the flame within guide you forward. Ride your truth. Draw your bow. The horizon is your altar, with the energy of freedom, fortune, and philosophy. You are the vision in motion. Sagittarius lives to become.

Sacred Reflection

What does freedom mean to me when it is no longer about escape? Describe what it feels like to follow joy instead of urgency. How can expansion begin within? Where is your soul asking you to leap — not to run, but to remember your sacred fire?

Ritual

Flames of Soul Illumination

Supplies
· Candles: white, purple, blue, green, orange, red, and black
· Parchment
· Oil for anointing

Flame 1: Sophia – The Flame of Divine Wisdom

"I am a soul woven of stars and memory."

Light the white candle and say aloud, *"I enter this rite not to seek power but to know myself beyond time. I call upon the flame of Sophia, wisdom of the soul, to guide my remembrance."*

Flame 2: Nous – The Flame of Higher Mind

"That which is above reflects within."

Light the purple candle. Invoke your higher self and soul council. Reflect on what sacred agreements you made beyond this incarnation. Gaze into the flame, and allow symbols, names, or lifetimes to rise.

Flame 3: Logos – The Flame of Soul Truth

"Truth is the song my soul remembers."

Light the blue candle. Speak or write this invocation: *"Show me the truth of this soul contract — its origin, its lesson, and its binding cord."*

Flame 4: Eros – The Flame of Heart Wisdom

"Love is the first vow and final liberation."

Light the green candle. Place your hands on your heart. Feel any emotional echoes — grief, joy, longing, or devotion from past life bonds. Say, *"If love is the teacher, let me receive the lesson. If pain is the path, let it now be transmuted."*

Flame 5: Mnemosyne – The Flame of Sacred Memory

"I awaken what has been forgotten."

Light the orange candle. Recall a specific memory, place, or figure from another lifetime connected to your current situation. Journal or draw it. Allow the fire to act as a scribe between worlds.

Flame 6: Ethos – The Flame of Choice and Courage

"I am not bound by the past — I choose again."

Light the red candle. Write on parchment the contract you wish to release or evolve. Say, *"I no longer serve this outdated contract. I release all karmic residue with courage and grace."* Burn the parchment in the red flame (or black, if you prefer full release).

Flame 7: Thanatos – The Flame of Shadow and Liberation

"Death is not the end, but transformation."

Light the black candle. In silence, reflect on what part of your identity or pattern you are ready to let die. Whisper, *"As this flame dances, so does my soul awaken. What was once hidden is now transmuted."*

Closing the Circle: Integration and Return

Snuff out each candle in reverse order with gratitude and presence. Anoint your third eye with oil, and place both hands on your heart. Say, *"I walk forward illumined by soul memory, guided by fire, and reborn in sovereign light. The work is done. So mote it be."*

Element: Earth

Ruling Planet: Saturn

House: Tenth (social status, career, ambition, legacy)

Essence: *Disciplined ✦ Ambition ✦ Legacy ✦ Reverent ✦ Sacred Structure*

Dragonfly Echo

I rise through rooted vision and lead with integrity. I honor the weight of my calling and build my future with sacred discipline. My boundaries are holy. My path is intentional. With patience and devotion, I anchor my magic into the world. My legacy is carved in stone and soul.

31. Capricorn: The Sea Goat

Energetic Invitation: Capricorn, the tenth sign of the zodiac, is governed by Saturn, the keeper of time, karma, and sacred architecture.

Represented by the sea goat, a mystical hybrid of deep-sea wisdom and mountain mastery, Capricorn invites you to merge grounded discipline with spiritual depth. It climbs slowly but with sovereign intention, knowing that every step and every choice builds something lasting.

This is not a sign of shortcuts but of sacred structure. It asks, What are you devoted to building that will outlive the moment?

Capricorn's path is legacy. Ruler of the tenth house of career, ambition, and public recognition, it beckons you to become the architect of your reality, to rise with honor, to build what is worthy, and to hold your boundaries like stone, not as walls, but as sacred shapes that protect your truth.

When Capricorn appears, you are being initiated into long-term commitment. Whether you are crafting a business, anchoring a new identity, or defining your life's work, this archetype says to show up and stay rooted. Let your effort be a form of devotion.

Here, sovereignty means owning your time, choices, and direction. Legacy is not built in urgency; it is etched in ritual, responsibility, and reverence. Discipline is not punishment; it is sacred promise.

Let your ambition be aligned with soul, not ego. Let the outer climb mirror your inner becoming. Saturn does not forget the effort you give. Your karma is woven with care. You are here to build more than a moment. You are here to last.

♑ Capricorn ♄

December 22 - January 19

Disciplined • Ambition • Legacy •
Reverent • Sacred Structure

December 22 – January 19

♑ Capricorn ♄

The Sea Goat

31

Shadow Path

Capricorn's shadow can surface as burnout, overcontrol, or fear-driven ambition. When structure becomes rigidity and discipline becomes depletion, the sea goat forgets its soul.

Are you measuring your worth by achievement, status, or others' expectations? Do your sacred goals now feel like cages of pressure? This calls for a softening, a pause, and I return to the why behind your work.

You are not a machine. Discipline without compassion is exhaustion. Sovereignty requires rest as much as it demands responsibility.

Capricorn's drive can become detached when it forgets its depths. Remember that sacred success honors spirit and structure equally. Let the climb be intentional, not punishing. Let your legacy be one of integrity, not just output.

Symbolic Vision: The sea goat appears in deep indigo, poised against a luminous green veil of cosmic consciousness. Its coiled, spiraling tail moves like memory, ancient and enduring, reminding us that time is not linear, but cyclical.

Its body balances two sacred truths: the grounded determination of earth and the intuitive depth of the sea. Capricorn is not *either/or* — it is both. This creature belongs to two worlds, and it honors both. It climbs, not to escape the depths, but to embody them.

Its horns arc toward the heavens like crescent moons sculpted from bone and starlight. These are not mere tools of defense — they are antennae tuned to ancestral law, spiritual authority, and cosmic order. They divine what is unseen, interpreting karma not as punishment, but as sacred contract. Saturn, Capricorn's ruler, governs karma and structure; it is the planet of time, accountability, and soul evolution. The glyphs of Capricorn and Saturn shine like seals across the sea goat's form — sigils of mastery earned through persistence.

Floating orbs drift nearby — messengers of spirit, casting quiet light upon the sea goat's path. They illuminate the dual essence of this archetype: one half tirelessly climbs toward legacy, public impact, and worldly responsibility, while the other half remembers the emotional and spiritual undercurrents that shape it. Capricorn's power lies in this duality — its ability to build real-world structures that remain rooted in unseen wisdom.

This is not an energy of haste or egoic striving. The sea goat is guided by sacred structure and builds slowly and intentionally with reverence. It does not reach for achievement for status alone; it creates in service to the greater whole. Discipline becomes devotion. Boundaries become blueprints. Sovereignty becomes the sacred right to shape one's own destiny, free from distortion or performance.

The tenth house, which Capricorn rules, represents our vocation, social standing, and enduring contribution. Here the inner calling crystallizes into visible impact. This is the apex of the chart, where the soul's quiet intention meets the world stage. The sea goat builds not for applause but for alignment with its divine task. It asks, What will outlast you? What are you crafting with your one, sacred climb?

Capricorn is the architect of legacy, the guardian of sacred time, and the living expression of karma earned through effort. In its gaze, time is not an enemy but a teacher. It builds with integrity and with reverence for each stone laid. Every action is infused with intention. Every climb is a sacred ritual. This is how foundations are formed that endure lifetimes.

Capricorn remembers. Capricorn endures. Capricorn builds and never ceases their climb. Capricorn builds with intention and rises with integrity.

Sacred Reflection

In what ways have structure and discipline supported my growth, and where have they become cages? Reflect on how you can bring more compassion and flexibility into the systems within which you live and work without sacrificing your goals or sovereignty.

Ritual

The Legacy of Stone and Soul

Supplies
- A small glass jar with a lid
- Herbs: rosemary (protection), sage (clarity), or thyme (devotion)
- Crystals: black tourmaline (boundaries), garnet (commitment), or smoky quartz (grounding)
- A small amount of salt or soil
- Pen and paper
- Optional: wax or black or brown string to seal the jar

Step 1: Construct the Sacred Foundation.

Prepare your space by cleansing it physically and energetically. Lay out your tools in a grounding circle. Place your hands over the jar and whisper, *"This vessel becomes the keeper of my structure and soul, a guardian of intention, and a shrine to discipline."*

Step 2: Invoke the Sea Goat.

Stand with steady posture, breathe deeply, and call in the Capricorn archetype. Say, *"Capricorn, guide of sacred time, sea goat of strength, mountain and ocean combined. I invoke your wisdom and sovereign grace. Help me carve a path that time cannot erase."* Visualize a spiral of ancient, earthen energy rising through your spine. Feel the presence of the sea goat beside you — steadfast, silent, and wise.

Step 3: Write the Legacy Intention.

On a piece of paper, write your intention — something you are committed to build over time, rooted in integrity and aligned with your soul. This could be a sacred goal, a spiritual vow, or a long-term path. Begin with the phrase, *"I build with intention...."* Fold the paper toward you, and place it in the bottom of the jar to set the foundation.

Step 4: Layer the Elements of Devotion.

Add your spell ingredients one by one into the jar: a pinch of salt or soil to ground the work, the herbs while naming their powers (e.g., rosemary for sacred protection), and the crystals, charging each with your energy. As you layer say aloud, *"Each layer is laid with devotion. Each piece is a step on my path. With patience, I ascend."*

Step 5: Seal the Jar with Saturn's Blessing.

Firmly close the lid. Wrap black or brown string around the lid, and tie three knots while repeating, *"Bound by time; blessed by Saturn; sealed with sacred structure. So it is."* If using wax, drip it over the lid, and inscribe the Capricorn glyph or Saturn symbol as a seal of power.

Step 6: Ground and Anchor the Jar.

Sit on the ground, and hold the completed spell jar in your hands. Visualize roots growing from the jar deep into the earth. Say, *"This spell is steady. This spell is mine. Through every season and test of time. What I build, I bless. What I plant, I tend. Let this magic endure without end."*

Step 7: Placement and Stewardship

Place your spell jar in a sacred or visible location: an altar, work desk, or near your journal. Let it serve as a daily reminder of your path. Touch it when you feel doubt, burnout, or misalignment. Revisit and recharge it monthly, or every Saturday, to reinforce your devotion and legacy.

Element: Air

Ruling Planet: Uranus (modern), Saturn (traditional)

House: Eleventh (house, community, innovation, soul purpose)

Essence: *Conscious Flow*
✦ *Independent* ✦ *Visionary*
✦ *Eccentric* ✦ *Uncertainty*
✦ *Revolutionary* ✦
Humanitarian

Dragonfly Echo

I think freely, feel deeply, and channel light into the future. I am the idea before it is known and the signal of change. My uniqueness is sacred. I dare to be different. I move the stagnant and light the way for others to awaken their own truth.

32. Aquarius: The Water Carrier

Energetic Invitation: Aquarius, the eleventh sign of the zodiac, arrives as a disruptor, liberator, and visionary guide. It is ruled by Uranus — the planet of sudden change, cosmic intelligence, and future thought — and traditionally by Saturn, the architect of order and time. Aquarius bridges the radical and the responsible. This dual rulership births an energy that is both wildly inventive and deeply aware of its soul purpose.

Symbolized by the water carrier, Aquarius carries consciousness, not emotion. The water they pour is made of thought, code, and vision — an uncontainable current of awakened awareness. It flows into the collective, activating new frequencies. This is conscious flow. When Aquarius appears, it's not just a call to dream—it's a call to redesign.

Aquarius rules the eleventh house, the domain of community, soul groups, innovation, and aligned contribution. Here, individuality meets impact. Aquarius reminds you that you are not here to fit in but to free yourself and in doing so, free others.

You are invited to release outdated systems and step into uncertainty with clarity. What once made you feel strange may now be your greatest wisdom. Eccentricity becomes medicine. Independence becomes prophecy.

You are the signal in the static. Let your uniqueness lead. Let your truth ripple. Aquarius does not fear difference — it is the embodiment of new codes rising. You are here to reimagine the world. Trust the frequency. Pour it forward.

≈ Aquarius ♄

January 20 - February 18

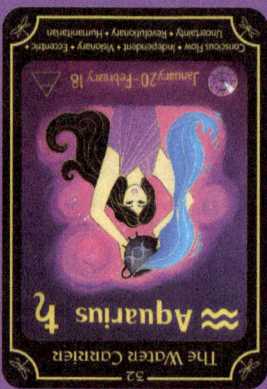

Shadow Path

Aquarius may reflect disconnection, dissociation, or rebellion without purpose. The water carrier's flow can stagnate into isolation or intellectual superiority, rejecting others before risking vulnerability.

Are you dimming your truth to blend in or resisting collaboration in fear of losing your uniqueness? Both extremes distort your path. This reversal invites you to reconnect to your why.

Aquarius can also fall into visionary overload. The future may feel so far ahead that the present becomes untended. You may become stuck defending outdated ideals under the illusion they are progressive.

This reversal asks, Are you flowing into the future, or are you stuck defending the past? Your originality is sacred. Let your uniqueness lead.

Symbolic Vision: Aquarius rules the eleventh house and invites us to activate our soul purpose in service to the greater whole. In this cosmic domain, community becomes a sacred container for transformation. Here innovation is not trend — it is truth breaking through limitation, a wave of future-encoded insight rippling into collective consciousness.

Although Aquarius is the water carrier, her element is air — the unseen force of thought, truth, and transmission. She does not pour water but cosmic intelligence, delivered through sacred frequency. Her gift is vision; her purpose is awakening.

A cosmic woman lifts a shimmering cauldron, pouring crystalline waves of knowledge into a violet galaxy — the future embodied and the sacred disruption. Aquarius stands robed in amethyst as a high priestess of star realms. The substance she pours is encoded vibration, shimmering with clarity, revelation, and divine knowing.

The cauldron represents her identity as a vessel of revolutionary truth, shaped by ancient wisdom and futuristic vision. Adorned with the triple moon, this sacred container links her to lunar mysteries and divine feminine power. Spirals behind her echo the cosmos — timeless, infinite, and alive with messages for those who listen. They whisper, *"You are more than this moment. You are the shift."*

Ruled by Uranus, the planet of disruption and awakening, Aquarius teaches us that uncertainty is not chaos — it is potential unformed. She does not fear the unexpected. She thrives in it. Her energy is eccentric, electric, unexpected —and undeniably prophetic.

Independent by nature, Aquarius is not here to fit in. She is here to challenge. Her mind moves beyond what is, seeking what could be. She sees the world not only as it is, but also as it might be if liberated from outdated systems. She embodies conscious flow, blending logic with instinct and intellect with soul.

She is the great visionary — a force of change, calling in new paradigms. Her ideas come not from convention but from ether, sky-scripted and starlit. She channels divine wisdom, bridging celestial insight and earthly action.

In the realm of Aquarius, freedom is sacred, collaboration is holy, and imagination is a portal. She reminds us to dream beyond borders, to question limits, and to align with causes that uplift the collective.

She is the oracle, the divine disruptor, and the cosmic pulse that stirs sleeping minds. With galaxies in her gaze and destiny on her lips, she asks, What hasn't been dreamed yet?

Sacred Reflection

What parts of myself have felt too strange for others to understand? Revisit those traits. Can you see them now as sources of wisdom or originality? How might your eccentricity be sacred?

Ritual

The Divine Disruptor

- Amethyst, clear quartz, or labradorite
- A violet or indigo candle
- An empty vessel or amphora (bowl, cup, or symbolic container)
- Lavender, mugwort, or incense for clearing
- Pen and journal or paper scroll
- A chime, bell, or tuning fork
- A small bowl of water (optional: charged under the moonlight)

Step 1: Clear the Signal.

Light your incense or herbs. Sweep the smoke around your body, crown, and third eye. Ring the bell or tuning fork to vibrate the air around you. Breathe deeply and say, *"I clear the air. I open the channel. I release noise and receive signal."* Envision your mind becoming quiet, spacious, and radiant like starlight.

Step 2: Light the Cosmic Flame.

Light the violet or indigo candle, connecting with the archetype of the water carrier. Gaze into the flame and say, *"I light the fire of insight. I awaken my star-born mind. I welcome the frequency of future truth."*

Step 3: Embrace Your Inner Eccentric.

Write or say aloud three ways you are beautifully different, unconventional, or ahead of your time. Then affirm, *"My difference is divine. I honor my originality as a gift to the world."* Wrap yourself in a fabric or item that expresses your individuality. Dress as the oracle you are.

Step 4: Channel the Future.

Hold your crystal, and place your hand over your third eye or crown. Close your eyes and ask, *"What is the idea that wants to come through me now?"* Allow visions, phrases, or feelings to emerge. Write down whatever flows without editing. This is sacred transmission.

Step 5: Pour the Offering.

Hold your symbolic vessel or cup. Speak aloud your insight, message, or intention as you slowly pour water into the bowl (or simply move your hands as if pouring frequency into the air). Say, *"I offer this transmission to the future. I pour my light into the stream of awakening."* Imagine your truth rippling out through the quantum field, touching those who are ready.

Step 6: Connect with the Eleventh House Frequency.

Visualize a web of light connecting you to kindred souls across space and time — those who also carry future codes. Say aloud, *"I am not alone. I am part of a greater vision. I awaken with others who dream beyond the now."* Feel the presence of soul-aligned allies, even if you have not met them yet.

Step 7: Integrate the Shift.

Journal your answers to the following questions:
- *What truth did I access in this ritual?*
- *How will I embody this vision moving forward?*
- *What outdated belief am I ready to disrupt?*

Close your ritual by blowing out the candle and ringing your bell once more. Say, *"I am the sacred vessel. I am the oracle. I carry the current of change. The future flows through me."*

Element: Water

Ruling Planet: Neptune (modern), Jupiter (traditional)

House: Twelfth (dreams, subconscious, secrets, spirituality)

Essence: *Dreamer ✦ Mystic ✦ Unpredictable ✦ Imagination ✦ Temperamental ✦ Creative ✦ Escape*

Dragonfly Echo

I am the dreamer and the deep seer. I soften, surrender, and merge with Source. I trust the tides of my inner knowing and swim through realms of magic, emotion, and spirit. I listen beyond logic and flow with soul. I am guided by visions, healed by mystery, and returned to the sacred sea within.

33. Pisces: The Fish

Energetic Invitation: The sacred dreamer of the deep, Pisces is the veil-thinner of the zodiac and the final sign in the spiral — a mystic who swims between worlds, dissolving the seen and unseen.

Guided by Neptune's oceanic currents and blessed by Jupiter's spiritual breadth, Pisces flows with romantic vision and intuitive depth. It holds the compass of the twelfth house, the domain of dreams, soul wisdom, and all that moves beneath the surface.

This card invites you to surrender — not to drift, but to remember. Here imagination is not an escape; it is a sacred expression. Let the illusions fall away and the unseen rise. You are being called into your mystical nature, to feel and to know without needing proof. The inner landscape of your subconscious is alive with symbols. In stillness, dreams speak, and your role is to listen.

Pisces embodies the beauty of temperamental waters — fluid, emotional, and ever-changing. This is not instability; it is sensitivity refined into wisdom. You are the dreamer and the channel, the soft strength that heals with compassion, and the visionary who senses what others miss.

Your soul may long for sacred practices that engage art, music, poetry, or spiritual care. Follow them. Let them open portals to your truth. You are not broken or lost — you are in sacred initiation.

You are a vessel for dreamwork and a mirror of divine care. Let your intuition lead you into mystery. This is sacred softness, not fragility. You are Pisces — born of water, ruled by stars, and shaped by the unseen.

Pisces

♓ ♃

February 19 – March 20

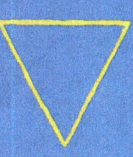

Shadow Path

When Pisces slips into shadow, the sacred waters turn cloudy. You may feel emotionally overwhelmed, entangled in illusion, or caught in fantasies that separate you from reality. Your sensitive nature may absorb emotions that are not yours, making it hard to find your own center.

Are you drifting from truth in favor of escape? Are you losing yourself in the needs of others? This moment asks for a gentle return. Anchor your compassion with clarity. Let your intuition illuminate rather than obscure. Spiritual connection is not avoidance; it is presence.

Removing delusion does not destroy the dream; it reveals its deeper truth. As distortion dissolves, your intuition rises strong and sure. Follow it. It is the current that carries you back to your soul's truth.

Symbolic Vision: In a sea of layered blues — deep indigo, aquamarine, and twilight mist — two swirling fish swim in opposite directions, bound by invisible threads of memory and moonlight. Their movement is timeless and spiraled, echoing the sacred geometry of the soul. This is not linear motion; it is the dance of eternity.

With each flick of their tails, they awaken ancient tides. The surface of the water ripples with moonlit reflection, casting visions of past lives, quiet longings, and the shimmering edge of futures still forming.

Pisces lives at the threshold of the seen and the unseen, with one foot in this world and one in the luminous unknown. It is the artist of the zodiac — the dream painter, the feeling sculptor, the melody weaver. To Pisces, intuition is more than a whisper — it is a current that carries truth beneath the surface. It listens with the heart, speaks in symbols, and loves in a language beyond logic.

Pisces is ruled by Neptune, a cosmic compass for dreams, illusions, and transcendence. Neptune is about what we imagine and what we forget. It tempts us to escape, but Pisces teaches that real freedom is not found in retreat, but in clarity. When illusion dissolves, truth surfaces like a pearl. And from that truth, art is born.

Co-ruled by Jupiter, Pisces holds sacred insight, divine empathy, and the gift of spiritual generosity. It opens wide to love that expects nothing in return. It is at once temperamental and tender — a healer who feels the wound and sings the remedy. With a sigh, prayer, or song, Pisces brings balm to soul fractures.

It is no surprise that Pisces rules the twelfth house — the celestial sanctuary of secrets, solitude, dreams, healing, and divine communion. In this liminal temple, silence is sacred and surrender is initiation. Here boundaries blur and the soul remembers where it came from. Endings do not signal closure; they mark transformation.

Elemental water gives Pisces its depth, fluidity, and psychic sensitivity. But this water is not still — it moves with feeling, intuition, and internal knowing. Pisces can be both romantic and moody, mystical and elusive, compassionate yet mysterious. It carries the wisdom of the subconscious and the shimmer of the unseen.

Let your imagination serve as your compass. Let your tears cleanse what must be released. Let your dreams offer sacred direction. You are the mystic, the visionary, and the vessel of divine wonder. When the tides rise, do not resist. Float, and let the current guide you home.

Sacred Reflection

What symbols or dream images have recently visited me, and what deeper truths might they hold? Have you witnessed anything in meditation, dreams, or nature that felt like a message? What inner knowledge is ready to be unlocked?

Ritual

The Dream Body and Intuitive Flight

Supplies

- *Amethyst,and labradorite*
- *Mugwort, lavender, or frankincense (optional: singing bowl)*
- *Dream journal*
- *Blue or silver candle*
- *Lavender oil*
- *Audio track for binaural beats or oceanic soundscapes*

Step 1: Create Your Dream Temple.

Cleanse the area with smoke from mugwort, lavender, or frankincense, or use a singing bowl to shift the frequency. Place an amethyst beneath your pillow to clarify visions or labradorite for dreamwalking and astral travel. Dim the lights, and anoint your third eye and heart with lavender oil. This is your vessel of entry.

Step 2: Cast the Circle of Sleep.

Lie down or sit with intention. Close your eyes, and visualize a glowing indigo or silver-blue circle of light forming around your bed — soft, shimmering, and protective. This is your sacred field. Breathe rhythmically, inhaling for four counts, holding for four, and exhaling for six. Repeat until your energy calms and expands. Visualize the veil thinning like mist, parting to reveal the realm between worlds.

Step 3: Call in the Dreamweaver.

Invoke Pisces' dreamweaver archetype or your own astral guides and spirit allies. As your awareness shifts, softly say: *"Spirit of the dreamweaver, I call to you. Open the gates of night, and show me what is true. Wrap me in your silver strands of light, and carry me beyond the veil tonight."* Trust the shift. Feel the tingling and the soft stirring. Pisces opens the intuitive gateway.

Step 4: Set Your Dream Spell.

Say your sacred intention aloud. For intuitive guidance try, *"Tonight I trust my inner knowing. My dream speaks truth."* Write this, and place it under your pillow or in your journal. Let Pisces' intuitive current amplify your purpose.

Step 5: Activate the Gateway.

Play binaural beats, oceanic sounds, or chant gently, *"I drift, I dream, I rise, and I fly."* Repeat seven times. Gaze into your candle or crystal, letting the edges of waking blur. You are now at the threshold.

Step 6: Surrender to the Veil.

Lie down, close your eyes, and receive. Notice flickers of light, imagery, or sensation. If you feel a floating sensation, embrace it. Pisces governs surrender through feeling. Say, *"I am safe. I am aware. I am free."*

Step 7: Anchor and Record.

Upon waking, stay still. Ask, What did I see? What did I feel? Record every detail — symbols, sensations, colors, and even silence. Pisces speaks in layers. This is how you build your intuitive archive. Close by saying, *"I honor the realms I have traveled. I return whole, wise, and protected."*

34. Celtic Wheel of Life

Essence

Sabbats
Nature's Mirror
Sacred Wheel
Seasonal Wisdom

Dragonfly Echo

I walk the spiral path of time. I honor what rises, what falls, and what waits in the quiet between. I am never lost; I am cycling home. I trust in sacred natural transitions and the rhythm of the seasons. I move with the Sabbats, honoring each spiritual threshold and transition as a magical step in my unfolding.

Energetic Invitation: The Celtic Wheel of the Year is more than a calendar — it is a sacred mirror, reflecting both the Earth's movement and the soul's evolution. This ancient rhythm pulses through eight turning points: Imbolc, Ostara, Beltane, Litha, Lammas, Mabon, Samhain, and Yule. These Sabbats were originally woven into agricultural and seasonal rites — moments when the land itself guided how we lived, worked, celebrated, and rested.

Long before the concept of a wheel emerged, these sacred thresholds were already honored in alignment with the solstices, equinoxes, and natural shifts in light and fertility. The term "Wheel of the Year" came later, offering language to describe a truth our ancestors lived intuitively: Life unfolds in sacred cycles, not straight lines.

Each spoke of the wheel holds an energy: a call to sow, bloom, reap, or release. To walk this path is to move in spiral rhythm, not rushing toward completion but attuning to life's organic unfolding. When this card arrives, you are asked, Where are you now? Are you in descent or renewal? Are you ready to act or being called to listen and allow?

The wheel reminds you that you are not separate from nature — you are nature. You are the wheel, moving through seasons of becoming and undoing. Your soul rises like Beltane fire, rests like winter frost, and dreams like the waning moon. Trust this spiral path. Let the sacred wheel hold you. You are part of Earth's story, turning through time with grace.

Shadow Path

When reversed, this card speaks to a disconnection from sacred rhythm — a reluctance to honor your season. Perhaps you are clinging to growth when stillness is needed or rushing toward light when your soul calls for quiet descent. In resisting a natural transition, you stall your own unfolding. This is not a failure but a moment to realign.

You may feel the urge to push forward, bypass rest, or avoid what feels like an ending. Yet every season has purpose. In shadow, the wheel teaches that forcing movement disrupts divine timing. Endings are not mistakes; they are initiations.

Release the illusion of linear arrival. Trust the spiral. All things shift in sacred rhythm. Let the wheel turn. The cycle will carry you when you surrender, not when you strive.

Symbolic Vision: The Wheel of the Year turns through eight sacred thresholds, each a mirror of Earth's rhythm and the soul's unfolding. These festivals are not linear steps but spirals of remembrance, reflection, and renewal.

Imbolc awakens the soul from winter's slumber. The sacred flame of Brigid flickers gently, calling forth purification and quiet emergence. Her woven cross offers protection and whispers of the life yet to bloom.

Ostara arrives on the spring equinox, when light and shadow stand in balance. Fertility stirs the land as blossoms open and bunnies play — symbols of innocence and new beginnings. This is a time of planting dreams and embracing joyful rebirth.

Beltane ignites the fires of passion and sacred union. Blossoms crown the maypole as ribbons spiral upward. Blackbirds call from the thinning veil, inviting us to dance with desire, creativity, and soul-deep connection. This is the festival of wild magic and ecstasy.

Litha, the summer solstice, celebrates the longest day. The bee hums its golden hymn, gathering sweetness in devotion. This is the season of full bloom, when purpose ripens and joy radiates from every petal. Drink deeply from the light.

Lammas marks the first harvest. Beneath amber skies, we honor the sacred exchange of effort into abundance. A priestess stands in the fields with arms full of grain — a living altar of gratitude. This is the time to give thanks and offer back.

Mabon, the autumn equinox, brings reflection. Cauldrons simmer at the hearth as day and night meet again. Twin brooms stand as guardians of reciprocity and release. Here we honor what has been gathered and what is ready to fall away.

Samhain opens the gate to the unseen. A skull rests upon the altar, honoring the ancestors. The veil thins, and spirits draw near. This is the witch's new year — a sacred descent into memory, mystery, and communion with what lingers in shadow.

Yule, the winter solstice, arrives with hush and hope. The Holly King watches over the longest night, cloaked in evergreen and crowned in frost. Within this stillness, light is reborn. Rest, dream, and trust: The sun shall rise again.

Together these Sabbats form the Sacred Wheel — a spiraling path of becoming, releasing, and returning. As it turns, so do you. You are not separate from the seasons. You are the wheel — living, breathing, and transforming with every turn of light and shadow.

Sacred Reflection

Which Sabbat energy resonates with my current state of being? This question aligns your soul with the rhythm of the Celtic year, helping you locate where your energy mirrors the greater wheel — whether you are sowing, blooming, harvesting, or resting.

Ritual

A Ceremony of Cycles, Balance, and Renewal

Supplies

- *A small wheel or circle (wooden, woven, or drawn on paper)*
- *Green, gold, and white candles (representing Earth, Sun, and Spirit)*
- *A sprig of oak or ivy (symbolizing endurance and renewal)*
- *A bowl of water and a pinch of salt*
- *A crystal for cycles and transitions (moonstone, labradorite, or citrine)*
- *The Celtic Wheel of Life oracle card*
- *A pen and journal or parchment*

Step 1: Create Sacred Space.

Begin by casting your circle. Place the bowl of water with salt in the center, and breathe deeply. Whisper, *"I call upon the turning wheel — the seasons, the cycles, and the balance of life."*

Step 2: Light the Quarter Flames.

Arrange the candles around your circle:
- Green in the north (earth, grounding)
- Gold in the east (air/light, inspiration)
- White in the south (fire/spirit, transformation)

Light each candle, calling the energy of its direction into your ritual.

Step 3: Place the Oracle at the Hub.

Lay the Celtic Wheel of Life oracle card at the center of your circle. Gaze upon it as if it were a compass, and say, *"As the wheel turns, so do I. I honor each season of my soul."* Set a clear intention for this season. What are you calling in or letting go? Speak it from the heart.

Step 4: Conduct Elemental Blessing.

Dip your fingers in the salted water, and touch your brow, heart, and hands. Visualize balance flowing into you. Place the oak or ivy sprig across the Celtic Wheel of Life card as a blessing of nature's eternal rhythm.

Step 5: Use Crystal for Alignment.

Hold the crystal to your heart. Imagine it glowing with moonlight and sunlight, weaving the eternal dance of beginnings and endings. Whisper aloud your intention for this cycle.

Step 6: Perform Sacred Writing.

On your parchment, write:
- What season of life do you feel you are in now (e.g., sowing, tending, harvesting, resting)?
- What are you ready to release as the wheel turns?
- What are you are ready to invite as the new season emerges?

Step 7: Seal the Turning.

Safely hold your parchment over the candles' glow, and say, *"The wheel turns. I honor the past, embrace the present, and step into the unfolding future with grace."* Fold the parchment, and place it under the card or crystal until the next seasonal shift.

Closing intention: Blow out the candles in reverse order. Thank the Celtic wheel for guiding your steps. End by saying, *"So the wheel turns; so my life flows. Blessed be."*

Essence
Portals
Clairvoyance
Magical Essence
Shimmering Shift
Transformation

Dragonfly Echo

I call upon the shimmer between worlds. I shed illusion and rise in truth. With translucent wings like the dragonfly, I let light pass through me. I glide with grace, trust the unseen, and embody the magic I was born to live. Cloaked in magic, crowned in clarity, I am the witch in flight — mystic, radiant, and ever-unfolding.

35. Dragonfly

Energetic Invitation: The Dragonfly is a sacred messenger of transformation — swift, radiant, and multidimensional. Its iridescent wings shimmer with the wisdom of lifetimes, whispering truths through movement and light.

When Dragonfly appears, the shift has already begun. Change is no longer coming — it is here, gliding softly on translucent wings. You are being invited to evolve, not through struggle but through presence, breath, and grace.

This winged guardian symbolizes metamorphosis, emerging from its watery nymph stage into the air with newfound perspective. Like Dragonfly, you are transitioning between worlds — between the old self and the becoming. This reflects not only personal growth but also the sacred cycles of life, death, and spiritual rebirth.

Dragonfly's ability to reflect and refract light makes it a revealer of illusions. It helps you see beyond appearances and into deeper truths. In Navajo teachings, it is the keeper of pure waters, reminding you to cleanse the spirit and honor clarity.

Its flight is agile, joyful, and precise — a dance of lightness and strength. Dragonfly teaches you to live in the present moment, to cherish the ephemeral beauty of life, and to face challenges with courage.

As a bridge between water and sky, Dragonfly connects you to both earth and spirit. It delivers messages from the unseen, reminding you that you are not alone. Shed old narratives. Trust the unfolding. You are no longer who you were. You are becoming — clearer, lighter, and deeply aligned with truth.

Shadow Path

When reversed, Dragonfly reflects a hesitation to change — a reluctance to shed what no longer fits. You may be grasping tightly to old identities, illusions, or comforts, fearing what will arise in their absence. The illusion of safety may be stronger than your trust in transformation. Yet truth does not wait for certainty. Dragonfly urges you to explore what you are resisting. Is it vulnerability? Surrender? The unknown shape of your becoming?

There is no need to force clarity, but do not deny the movement. Even stillness can be a disguise for fear. Let go, not in panic but in quiet power. Release with tenderness.

You are not falling apart — you are falling open. Let what no longer serves dissolve. The truth will find you in the letting go. You are already becoming. Trust the shimmer within.

Symbolic Vision: A golden dragonfly glides across a black void, its wings aglow with iridescent dimensions — each a shimmering whisper from the unseen. Suspended between realms, this luminous being is not simply flying; it is traversing portals of transformation, bridging timelines, and opening windows between the worlds.

Between its delicate antennae rests the ancient and steady eye of protection, a guardian sigil that deflects harmful intentions and dissolves distortion before it can reach your sacred field. This is more than a symbol; it is a spell of truth and safety.

The dragonfly is the embodiment of a shimmering shift — fluid, magical, and multidimensional. It does not declare change; it becomes it. Hovering at the edge of perception, it moves in spirals of subtle power. Its path is prophecy in motion. It shows us that transformation does not always come through force but often through grace, presence, and trust. The dragonfly invites you to embody your own magical essence, feel your way through the fog, and follow the glint of soul truth.

With wings that reflect the full spectrum of light, the dragonfly cuts through illusion. Its flight teaches that truth is not always bold or loud. It flickers through the quiet, between the breath and beneath the stories we have outgrown.

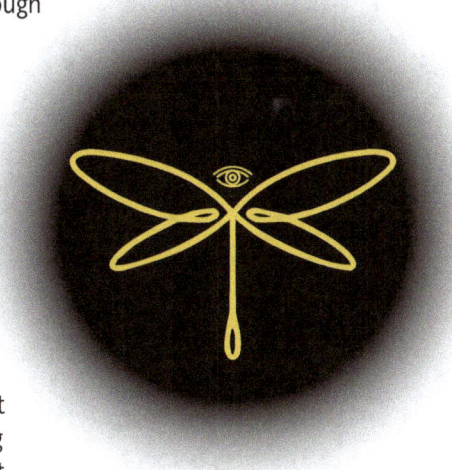

In its movement is the energy of clairvoyance and liminal sight. The dragonfly sees beyond the veil, carrying the whispers of spirit and the knowing of the ancient self. You are not just witnessing this vision — you are a part of it.

You are the prophecy — the light-body traveler who remembers. Within you lives wisdom from lifetimes before, encoded in your bones, breath, and being.

You are the one who shapes timelines with intention. In every moment you are free to choose again. You are never trapped. You are always spiraling — upward, inward, and onward — into deeper knowing and brighter becoming.

Dragonfly calls forth your highest truth and asks you to live from the soul — not someday, but now. You are not bound by what has been. You are the flicker of awakening and the living magic in motion. As you align with this sacred invitation, let your light shimmer without apology.

This is your mirror and your message: You are the spell. You are the sparkle. You are the dragonfly in flight, dancing between dimensions with elegance and courage. Trust your transformation. It is already underway.

Sacred Reflection

What symbolic images or dreams keep returning, and what do they mean? Write about recurring symbols, visions, or dream fragments. What archetypes, memories, or energies feel embedded within them? Let the visions/dreams be your soul guide.

Ritual

Accessing Dreamtime Akashic Insights

- Candle of your choice
- Herbs or resin of mugwort, sandalwood, or frankincense
- Crystals: labradorite, amethyst, smokey quartz
- Dragonfly talisman
- Journal

Step 1: Create a Sacred Sleep Temple.

Begin about 30 minutes before bed. Clear your physical space. Light a candle or incense (mugwort, sandalwood, or frankincense are ideal). Arrange sacred items: labradorite or amethyst crystals, a dream journal, and a dragonfly talisman to represent etheric flow. Dim the lights. Play soft ambient music, or sit in silence. Whisper, *"Tonight I enter sacred space. My dreamtime becomes a bridge between lives and timelines."*

Step 2: Ground and Seal with Intention.

Sit or lie down, and take three slow grounding breaths. Visualize your root chakra anchoring into the Earth and your crown extending to the stars. Say, *"I call upon my highest self, Akashic Record keepers, guides of light, and soul memory. I am ready to receive wisdom from all lifetimes that support the choice before me. May only what serves my evolution enter this space."*

Step 3: Activate the Akashic Key.

Place your dominant hand on your heart and your nondominant hand on your third eye. Visualize a golden spiral unfolding, revealing a luminous library or portal of light. Imagine a glowing book labeled with your soul's name. Affirm, *"I open the record of my soul. I access the truth of who I have been, who I am, and who I am becoming."*

Step 4: State Your Soul Question.

Whisper or write your question clearly and from the heart.
For example, *"What path aligns with my soul's highest good? What past-life wisdom can guide my choice?"* Place this question beneath your pillow or beside your heart.

Step 5: Drink the Dream Elixir.

Sip a tea that enhances dream recall, such as mugwort, blue lotus, or chamomile. As you drink, imagine your clairvoyance awakening. Affirm, *"As I sleep, I remember. As I dream, I receive. As I wake, I integrate."*

Step 6: Drift Into Dream with Invocation.

As you close your eyes silently repeat, *"Tonight I fly beyond the veil. Reveal who I have been so I may choose who I become. I open to soul truth, safely held in light."* Allow yourself to surrender into the dream realm.

Step 7: Integrate in the Morning.

Upon waking, journal all sensations, symbols, and fragments. Ask yourself, What did I feel or recognize? What wisdom surfaced? What feels clearer today? End by thanking your guides and affirming, *"I walk with wisdom across lifetimes. I choose with clarity and trust."*

Essence

Quintessence

Sacred Seal

Quantum

Aether

Magical Key

Ancient Codes

Dragonfly Echo

As above, so below. This sigil is my sacred seal. It unlocks ancient codes of magic within me. Through the power of quintessence, I align. I impress my intention into the quantum field. I am the channel. I am the spark. So let it be.

36. The Sigil

Energetic Invitation: The key to quintessence to awaken the ancient codes of magic through the power of the quintessence sigil is to step boldly into the field of miracles and sacred creation. This card is your invitation to imprint intention upon the universe — not with force, but with precise, sacred artistry.

You are not merely drawing a symbol; you are opening a portal. Sigils are magical blueprints — symbols crafted to embody a specific desire, purpose, or transformation. They act as bridges between the conscious and subconscious realms, embedding your intention deep into the energetic field, where manifestation begins.

In magic, a sigil is not just a design — it is a spell. Each curve holds current. Each stroke holds power. When activated, a sigil communicates your will to the unseen. It anchors desire into energy and energy into form. Your breath becomes part of the ritual. Your presence ignites the field. The fifth element — quintessence — spirals through the design, bringing Spirit into matter.

Used for love, healing, protection, or abundance, sigils are among the most versatile tools of the craft. But here you are not working from someone else's glyph. You are called to create your own, drawn from soul and shaped by intent. What you craft now is not simply art. It is alchemy.

Let your symbols echo the sacred codes still sleeping in your bones. Let them rise and speak. You are the magician and the message. This is your key.

Now is the time: Cast your intention, draw your truth, and seal your spell.

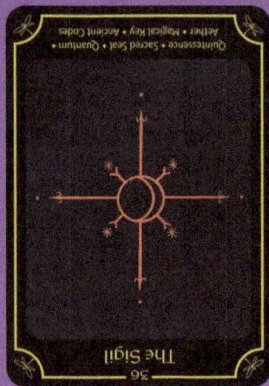

The Sigil
36

Shadow Path

When the Sigil appears reversed, it may reflect a disconnect from the sacred origin of your power. Are you casting without clarity or going through motions without meaning?

A sigil is not merely a symbol — it is a sealed energetic transmission. If your spell feels flat, revisit your alignment. Have you honored the soul behind the symbol?

This is a powerful moment to create a sigil not from desire alone but from the shadow you wish to transmute. Carve your fear into form. Let your doubt become the doorway. Place it into the quantum field with reverence, knowing transformation begins when truth is acknowledged.

The quantum field listens not only to your spell but also to your soul. Refine your intention. Redraw your power. You are still the key.

Symbolic Vision: The crescent moon glows as a whisper of magic — a sliver of light holding endless potential. This ancient curve is an amplifier of spells and a magnifier of desire. When drawn or invoked, it raises energy, enhances manifestation, and ignites your ritual into motion. Call upon it when you seek clarity, transformation, or heightened intention. Its shape speaks of what is just beginning to emerge — a promise on the horizon and a gateway to what is yet to bloom.

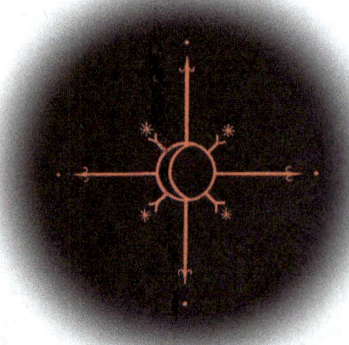

At the center of sacred space rests the circle — an unbroken line representing Spirit. It is the divine container, the cosmic womb, and the shield that holds what is holy. When you draw the circle, you are not just marking a boundary; you are invoking protection, completion, and the guidance of unseen forces. Use it to sanctify your spellwork, create energetic containers, and call upon the sacred to surround your workings.

The upward-pointing arrow, a witches' rune, channels force outward. It launches intention into the universe — a call to the cosmos. It is radiant with divine masculine energy, momentum, and purpose. Use this symbol when directing energy toward a specific manifestation, summoning external power, or declaring your will with boldness and clarity.

In contrast, the forked Y draws energy inward. It stirs the sacred feminine, intuition, and healing. This symbol speaks to the soul's depths, to the waters within, and to the inner wellspring of transformation. Use it for shadow work, self-reflection, and inner alignment.

The eight-pointed star is a glyph of mystery. It activates the portal of becoming — the space between knowing and unknowing. It symbolizes the magnetic pull of desire, the fire of dreams, and the dance with the unknown. Draw it to unlock hidden guidance, and trust what lies just beyond logic.

The dot is the focal point — the anchor. It is where your energy meets form and where your spell roots. All other lines flow to this center. It is clarity, presence, and purpose — the full embodiment of intention in the material world.

These symbols are powerful on their own, but your personal magic begins when you create. You are invited to craft your own sigil using the materials that speak to your spirit: charcoal, ink, thread, paint, chalk, embroidery, or even water drawn across sand. Each medium becomes an extension of your energy.

There are no rules, only resonance. Let your lines be spells. Let your shapes carry will. Let your hands become the brush of the divine.

Your sigil is your language. And in that sacred script, transformation begins.

Sacred Reflection

What color, shapes, line style, or pattern reflects my current emotional state, and how can I use them magically? Choose visual elements to match your mood: jagged for stress, flowing for ease, dotted for clarity. Could this become a code in your magical practice?

Ritual

Creating the Sacred
Script of Your Soul

Supplies

- A candle (white, silver, or color aligned with your intention)
- A bowl of salt or water (for grounding)
- A crescent moon symbol or charm (optional)
- Ink, charcoal, chalk, thread, paint, or pen
- Parchment, handmade paper, canvas, fabric, or natural surface (stone, wood, shell)
- Optional: crystals (clear quartz, selenite, or obsidian), incense of choice

Step 1: Create Sacred Space.

Light your candle, and cleanse your space with smoke or silence. Ground yourself by holding the bowl of salt or water. Breathe in deeply and say aloud, *"I open this space to sacred creation. I invite Spirit to move through symbol."* Visualize the circle of Spirit forming around you — whole, safe, and clear.

Step 2: Anchor Your Intention.

Place your hands over your heart, and speak your desire out loud. Be specific and speak in present-tense clarity. For example, *"I embody clarity and courage in all decisions."* Let this desire echo in your body.

Step 3: Choose Your Symbols.

Call in traditional archetypal symbols: the crescent moon for amplification and new beginnings; circle for spirit, protection, and sacred containment; arrow for outward energy and manifestation; forked Y for inner guidance, healing, and feminine flow; eight-pointed star for mystery, attraction, and divine portals; or dot for focus, grounding, and spell destination. You may choose any or all. Trust what resonates.

Step 4: Begin the Sigil Creation.

Using your chosen medium (e.g., ink, paint, chalk, or thread), begin drawing. Let your lines spiral, stretch, and flow intuitively. Let your hand move without overthinking. This is not art. This is spell. Allow new symbols to emerge. Repeat your intention mentally as you create.

Step 5: Breathe Life into the Sigil.

Place your palms over the finished symbol, and close your eyes. Visualize energy flowing into it — like moonlight into water or flame into wax. Say, *"This is my spell made visible. This is my power remembered."*

Step 6: Seal and Anchor.

Place a dot or mark to signify the spell's landing point. Let the sigil dry, settle, or rest overnight under moonlight or crystal. Optionally, keep it on your altar, burn it, bury it, or carry it with you.

Step 7: Close the Ritual.

Blow out the candle. Thank Spirit. Say, *"The spell is cast. The will is clear. So it is."* Carry the sigil forward with reverence — it is your sacred script, encoded with your truth and desire.

Lynn MagikCraft Swain's mission is to illuminate the sacred path within each person, guiding them to rise into higher consciousness, reclaim their truth, and explore their spiritual essence. She is a seventh-generation practitioner, psychic medium, tarot reader, and healer with close to 50,000 readings and sessions conducted worldwide.

As the founder of MagikCraft Bull City Magic, Magic on 70, MagikCraft Publishing, and the new podcast *Soul Goal by MagikCraft,* Lynn has guided thousands of people through profound transformation, intuitive awakening, and soul empowerment. She believes that everyone is psychic and that the soul already holds the answers we seek.

Expanding her own path of wisdom through Duke University Life and Career Coaching certification and Brian Weiss Past-Life Regression training, Lynn is also an avid seeker of knowledge, a devoted reader, and a collector of books and oracle and tarot decks. Her soul-centered work has been featured on or in collaboration with NBC, ABC, Duke University, the University of North Carolina, Giorgios Hospitality, Body Mind Spirit, Estée Lauder, Origins, *Indy Week,* A.R.E. (Edgar Cayce), and more — bringing her radiant teachings and sacred wisdom to audiences across the globe.

Transform your life today at MagikCraft.com!

 @MagikCraft ✦ lynn.magikcraft.swain.2025 ✦ @MagikCraft

Soul Goal by MagikCraft on Spotify and Apple podcasts

Stand in Your Power and Follow Your Soul Goal!